The So

Philip Metres

The Sound of Listening

**POETRY AS REFUGE
AND RESISTANCE**

UNIVERSITY OF MICHIGAN PRESS

Ann Arbor

Copyright © 2018 by Philip Metres
All rights reserved

This book may not be reproduced, in whole or in part, including illustrations,
in any form (beyond that copying permitted by Sections 107 and 108 of the
U.S. Copyright Law and except by reviewers for the public press), without
written permission from the publisher.

Published in the United States of America by the
University of Michigan Press
Manufactured in the United States of America
⊛ Printed on acid-free paper

A CIP catalog record for this book is available from the British Library.

Library of Congress Cataloging-in-Publication data has been applied for.

ISBN: 978-0-472-03728-5 (Paper : alk. paper)
ISBN: 978-0-472-12421-3 (ebook)

For Amy, Adele, and Leila: my refuge.

Acknowledgments

Thanks to the following journals and anthologies for publishing versions of these essays, sometimes with different titles:

A Sense of Regard: Essays on Poetry and Poetry (University of Georgia Press, 2015): "Carrying Continents in Our Eyes: Arab American Poetry after 9/11"

America: "Homing In: The Place of Poetry in the Global Digital Age"

Big Bridge: "*Lang/scapes*: War Resistance Poetry"

Cleveland Magazine: "By Heart: On Memorizing Poems," "Poetry as Refuge and Resistance"

Cross-Cultural Poetics: "'We Build a World': War Resistance Poetry in/as the First Person Plural"

Dispatches: "'The School among the Ruins': Reading Adrienne Rich on a Greyhound Bus"

Gulf Coast: "Erotic Soyuz: Twenty-Five Propositions on Translating (Arseny Tarkovsky)"

Jacket 2: "Parsing Arias: A Dialogue through 'abu ghraib arias' with Micah Cavaleri"

Kenyon Review: "(More) News from Poems: Investigative/Documentary/Social Poetics*"

Los Angeles Review of Books: "At the Borders of our Tongue: An Interview with Fady Joudah"

National Poetry Foundation: "Installing Lev Rubinstein's 'Farther and Farther On': From Note Cards to Field Walks"

Paideuma: from *"Poetry as Refuge and Resistance"*

PEN America: "The Pen Ten Interview with Philip Metres"

Poetry Foundation: "Beyond Grief and Grievance: Poetry after 9/11," "The News from Poetry: Investigative/Documentary/Social Poetics," and "Against a Cloistered Virtue: Poems for Peace"

Poetry and Popular Culture Blog: "Khalil Gibran: Local Boy Made Good"

Volta: "Poetry as Refuge and Resistance"

I've also borrowed language from "Behind the Lines" blog, *Behind the Lines: War Resistance on the American Homefront* (University of Iowa, 2007), "Poetry as Social Practice in the First Person Plural: A Dialogue on Documentary Poetics" with Mark Nowak (*Iowa Journal of Cultural Studies*), "'With Ambush and Stratagem': American Poetry in the Age of Pure War" (*The Oxford Handbook of Modern and Contemporary Poetry*, 2012), my afterword to *Tracking/Teaching: On Documentary Poetics* (Essay Press, 2015), and from various book reviews.

Thanks to Kazim Ali and Marilyn Hacker. Marilyn has been a keen encourager to so many whose voices would have been lost, and I include myself among that tribe of the margins. Kazim, also of that tribe, pushed me to go deeper. The book is better for their high standard.

Thanks as well to readers and editors: David Baker, Amy Breau, Danny Caine, Micah Cavaleri, Hayan Charara, Mike Chasar, Frank Giampietro, Jeff Gundy, Marilyn Hacker, Joe Harrington, Fady Joudah, Randa Jarrar, Paul Lauritzen, Dave Lucas, Fred Marchant, Khaled Mattawa, Laura McCullough, Mark Nowak, Caryl Pagel, Radius of Arab American Writers, Susan Schultz, Kim Stafford, Paige Webb (for the endnotes!), and Laura Wetherington. Thanks, finally, to John Carroll University, the Lannan Foundation, the National Endowment for the Arts, and the Ohio Arts Council, for their support of my writing.

Contents

Introduction

Poetry as Refuge and Resistance

At the end of 2016, in the wake of the election of Donald Trump, I found myself lying in a dark room in the middle of the day. I'd been lying there for days and would for many more after that.

What landed me in bed was absurd. Doing laundry in the basement of my sister's house, I'd hit my head. I hadn't been attacked by Trump supporters wielding a laundry machine or a drone shooting a laundry machine. No, the machine's glass door knocked me in the back of the skull as I leaned down into its hole to gather my daughter's wet shoes. I couldn't see straight, fumbled for words, and tunnel vision ensued. Later, at the ER, I was diagnosed with a concussion.

In that dark bedroom, lying to rest my aching brain, I was terrified. The very things that I would do in normal circumstances to calm myself I could not do: reading, listening to music, going for a run. Lit-up screens—from computers to televisions to laptop—left a ghost image in my head when I closed my eyes. I had no idea whether the damage would be permanent.

I did what most people do in dire circumstances: I resorted to prayer, reciting prayers I'd known since I was a child, puzzling over their strange phrases. *Give us this day our daily bread.* I started thinking about all the people I'd known who had suffered head injuries, suddenly kin to them, the tribe of the brain-addled. I listened to myself think. In that dark quiet, poetry came in fragments of phrases:

Like looking out
The wrong end of the telescope.
The wind, making a voice

Of everything in its way.
Ghost-halo at my third eye.
The sound of the dog barking
Rings the doorbell.

Line by line, my panic quieted. I was not entirely myself, but each phrase felt like a way to make a self again.

Then I remembered the end of Anton Chekhov's story "Gooseberries," in which Ivan shares with his traveling companions an anecdote about visiting his brother who had realized his dream of having a gooseberry farm. The gooseberries, however, were terribly bitter, and Ivan felt badly that he couldn't tell his brother the truth; he didn't want to spoil his happiness. Ivan then launches into a speech about happiness in a world of misery:

> There ought to be a man with a hammer behind the door of every happy man, to remind him by his constant knocks that there are unhappy people, and that happy as he himself may be, life will sooner or later show him its claws, catastrophe will overtake him—sickness, poverty, loss—just as he now neither sees nor hears the misfortune of others.[1]

Though I'd read the story many times, I couldn't help but think about the seething violence of that wish, to knock someone on the head. Ivan sounds like a frustrated radical. Of course, sometimes we'd like to knock some deluded people on the head. Some of us felt figuratively knocked in the head by Trump's election. Others, no doubt, will be knocked in the head, literally and figuratively, by Trump policies.

What Ivan had forgotten so easily was that, an hour earlier, after their long slog through the muddy Russian country, he and his friends had been washing in the river. Ivan splashed about in the water in sheer ecstasy, floating on his back, exclaiming "My God, my God!" He played so long that his friends finally had to yell at him to come out.

We need refuge, a place to be fully immersed in self-forgetful joy, if we want to resist injustice and oppression for the balance of our lives. Beside my bed in the dark, Rebecca Solnit's *Hope in the Dark* lay, a symbol of itself. Joy can be, in Solnit's words, "a fine initial act of insurrection."[2] We believe our age to be one of crisis, perhaps one of the worst ages. In this, it resembles every other age. We're afflicted with the illness of presentism, inflamed by digital media. Yes, it's true that there are real crises: global climate change, war and terrorism, racial oppression, predatory capitalism, sexual violence. But crisis thinking may be itself a sort of concussed thinking, causing us to fling ourselves at the latest distraction and lose our reason and empathy. Our empire and its echo chambers have made us terrified of terror, forgetful of our own histories of violence, and forgetful of our own need for peace.

In that dark room, nursing my head, poetry was a refuge, a way to return to myself, to remember other people who had suffered as I was suffering. In that dark room, freed from the blare and hammer of the "news," I thought: Trump does not exist. And in that dark room, he did not.

I had to leave that room in order to return to my life, but the dark room would be a refuge I had to return to, to come back to myself. It is the place from which I want to consider resistance. In light of the flurry of poetry activity constellating around the term "resistance," we need, more than ever, to consider the possibilities and limits of resistance. After twenty-five years of thinking and practicing a poetics of resistance, I have found myself oddly resistant to the sudden talk of resistance—as if resistance were merely a matter of hashtags or opposing Trump. After all, there was plenty to resist during the Obama Administration—drone strikes abroad, police killings of black people on the streets, Bashar al-Assad's massacre of civilians in Syria, bankers and predatory capitalists running amok around the globe, ongoing accrual of executive power, the buildup of a shadow security state—but these phenomena did not garner much widespread resistance.

This book attempts to provide a context for a poetics of resistance and refuge that predates the Trump Age and will be necessary long after it. In order to survive such moments, we need to glean the present and past for what might sustain us for the work ahead. *The Sound of Listening* gathers ten years of essays on poetry and builds on *Behind the Lines: War Resistance Poetry on the American Homefront, since 1941* (2007), staking a claim for the cultural work that a poem can perform—from providing refuge to embodying resistance, from recovering silenced voices to imagining and modeling a more just and peaceful world. Rather than delivering judgments of poetic taste, these essays are experiments in questioning and performances of possibility, an attempt to widen my own (and the reader's) listening and seeing. These essays ask: *What if X were poetry? And if poetry were Y?* I seek to claim spaces for both "tactical poetry" and "strategic poetry," as Thomas McGrath once termed them. For McGrath, tactical poems are often ephemeral works keyed to immediate events "without falling into political slogans," while strategic poems expand consciousness, untethered to a specific cultural or political moment—yet nonetheless invite us to change.[3]

While some essays in *The Sound of Listening* further explore the intersections between poetry and resistance, others inquire into movements in contemporary poetry that draw upon the world (documentary poetics), or literally draw on the world (*lang/scape* poetry, installation poetry) or draw us out into the world (translation, Arab American poetry, cosmopoetics, etc.). While I have always courted the idea of poetry as a rhetoric of resistance, I continue to return to the idea of poetry as fundamentally a kind of resistance itself—anti-rhetorical, a state anterior to positing. Poetry as the ground of opening into the possible. A refuge. Part of this shift is Slavoj Žižek's notion that resistance often can sustain the object of its critique; in other words, if our resistance is mere protest, it actually strengthens or even creates the system. The system can point to its tolerance of protest as proof of its beneficence, its openness, its justice. The other reason for this shift is my experience of poetry itself; the longer I write and read poetry, the more I'm intrigued by its irreducibility. Great poems seem great to me because something about them turns toward the ineffable. Great poems may confound or delight, teach or provoke—but they are great because their forms vibrate and resonate beyond political platforms, slogans, or formulae.

In other words, though we may feel the call to resist and write a poetry of resistance, perhaps we can learn from Chekhov's narrator in "Gooseberries," who manages both to witness to our political moment and the contradictions of our age and keep in mind the marathon of human liberation and planetary survival. Ivan, like all of us, sees life with partial sight; he is overwhelmed by the magnitude of human misery and deception, so much so that he wants happiness eradicated from the world, as if it were a disease. What he fails to consider (in addition to his own self-forgetfulness) is whether refuge, the refuge of delight, could be the very ground from which a politics can be built. Chekhov's unobtrusive narrators always remind me that to bear witness to the human struggle—and even our failures to understand our own condition—is a kind of love. Some poets, of course, do a good job knocking us about, trying to shake us awake to injustice, to spur us to act—one thinks of Amiri Baraka, Mahmoud Darwish, Bob Dylan, June Jordan, Adrienne Rich, Fady Joudah, Solmaz Sharif, Danez Smith, among others. Poets can be both scourgers and healers, alternately providing sting and balm; as Mother Jones once said about the work of social justice, our vocation is to comfort the afflicted and to afflict the comfortable.

The dialectic between refuge and resistance might explain why I was fascinated by the poetics of the Occupy Wall Street movement of 2011–2012. The Occupy movement did not waste its energies in rhetorical persuasion; the members of Occupy addressed themselves. W. B. Yeats once wrote that the quarrel with others makes rhetoric, but the quarrel with ourselves produces poetry. His poems are richly dialogical; "The Dialogue of Self and Soul," "Crazy Jane Talks with the Bishop," and "Easter 1916" vibrate with voices and positions. Great political poetry widens what Yeats meant when he talked about poetry as a struggle with our*selves.* Such poetry invites us to dilate our sense of the self in the first place. When speakers addressed Occupy at Zuccotti Park, people at the front would repeat what the speaker said so that those in the back would hear; it was a chorus, or a wave of choruses, called the Human Microphone. Eliminating the technologies of mass media meant that Occupy short-circuited the anti-war movement's damaging romance with media coverage. The point was building community, providing an autonomous zone, a refuge from the spotlight. And this leaderless movement was not interested in merely resisting the dominant culture or hammering out a list of demands; they wanted to create another world. For all

the obvious failures of Occupy to produce specific political re-
sults, Occupy's basic orientation—its utopian anarchism—felt,
at times, like the political correlative of poetry itself.

I'm interested increasingly in poetry and the arts as a way of
creating another life, of marking and embodying alternative
ways of being and living. As a way to explore the "theory/prac-
tice" dialectic, after each chapter that theorizes about a kind
of poetry (political elegy, Arab American poetry, documentary
poetry, lang/scape poetry, peace poetry, etc.), I narrow my focus
on exemplars: Adrienne Rich, Kahlil Gibran, the War Tax Resistance Committee, Lev Rubinstein, and Arseny Tarkovsky. Each
of these poets, facing conditions of marginality and oppression,
created and modeled other ways of being—for some, this meant
solitary being (Gibran, Tarkovsky), but for others (Rich, Rubinstein, the War Tax Resistance Committee), it meant being-in-
community, creating spaces for being together. The choice by
war resisters to refuse paying taxes is the most obvious example
of the overlap between these two orientations, between resistance and the poetics of living.

Finally, the dialogues that punctuate the book are an attempt
to model the dialogical at the heart of vital political poetry—
poems that include and amplify many voices but also enact a
kind of listening. Though Whitman once wrote, "I contain multitudes," I long for a poetry that breathes and seethes multitudes.
Talking with Randa Jarrar, Palestinian-American novelist, about
artistic freedom; or with Fady Joudah, Palestinian-American
poet and translator, about *Sand Opera*; or with Micah Cavaleri,
a veteran of the Iraq War, about the "abu ghraib arias" and the
war, challenged me to make sense of my own writing in light of
the insights of fellow writers.

The title also echoes the moment in William Stafford's "Traveling through the Dark," when the speaker must decide what
to do about the dead pregnant doe on a winding road at night.
As he considers the options, he notices: "around our group I
could hear the wilderness listen."[4] I love the weird loveliness of
that line, how the wilderness becomes personified and its listening becomes a kind of sound. In our noisy age, that moment is
primal. In this poem, the work of the poet is to regard the listen-

ing wilderness, to act in accordance with the larger (and largely nonhuman) architectures of the universe—even if he decides ultimately to preserve human safety.

Years ago, I heard a linguist surmise that the first word was *hist.* Listen. I can't prove his speculation, but it rhymed with what I love about language as it rises into poetry: it invites us to stop ourselves, in our bustle of noise, and dilate our senses—to another, to our surroundings—to selves wider than our selves. In "Homing In," I call *Sand Opera* "the sound of my listening"; I've come to think of that stance as both political and poetical, ethical and erotic, physical and spiritual. It is a discipline that I've spent my life trying to practice.

Perhaps it's true, as Seamus Heaney wrote, that "no lyric has ever stopped a tank."[5] But as Dave Lucas once noted, we don't know the futures that our poems create. Part of the problem is that the change is not always visible. We rarely know if a poem that someone read led them to oppose a war, protect a victim of sexual violence, or protest against a pipeline cutting through native land. The arts are part of the technologies of consciousness-change—often solitary, occasionally communal—but their work is mostly unseen. In this way, poetry and the arts resemble grassroots activism. As Solnit notes in her essay "The Angel of Alternate History,"

> most environmental victories look like nothing happened; the land wasn't annexed by the army, the mine didn't open, the road didn't cut through, the factory didn't spew effluents that didn't give asthma to the children who didn't wheeze and panic and stay indoors on beautiful days. They are triumphs invisible except by storytelling.[6]

We need writers to mark those moments, and those places, to tell us the history that has yet to be told. As Subcommandante Marcos has suggested, "We Indian peoples have resorted to the art of reading what has not yet been written."[7]

In "At the Un-National Monument along the Canadian Border," Stafford poses a parallel scenario to Solnit's invisible victories:

This is the field where the battle did not happen,
where the unknown soldier did not die.
This is the field where grass joined hands,
where no monument stands,
and the only heroic thing is the sky.

Birds fly here without any sound,
unfolding their wings across the open.
No people killed—or were killed—on this ground
hallowed by neglect and an air so tame
that people celebrate it by forgetting its name.[8]

Stafford's poem bears the sting of poignancy; he knows that the peace that has been won is so much more easily forgotten than the war and its blood sacrifice. Yet, the poem becomes its own monument to this place, where no stone markers need to commemorate those killed by war. The ripple effect of a good poem is the opposite of a bomb's concussion wave; it buoys us in its bracing music, whatever hurt it bears, holding us momentarily aloft, helping us to stand our ground, providing us a spark to make our way in the general dark.

Notes

1. Ralph Matlaw, ed., *Anton Chekhov's Short Stories* (New York: W. W. Norton, 1979), 193.

2. Rebecca Solnit, *Hope in the Dark: Untold Histories, Wild Possibilities* (Chicago: Haymarket Books, 2016), 25.

3. Thomas McGrath, "The Frontiers of Language," Modern American Poetry, accessed January 15, 2017, http://www.english.illinois.edu/maps/poets/m_r/mcgrath/tactical.htm

4. William Stafford, "At the Un-National Monument along the Canadian Border," *The Way It Is: New & Selected Poems* (St. Paul: Graywolf Press, 1998), 77.

5. Seamus Heaney, *The Government of the Tongue: Selected Prose, 1978–1987* (New York: Macmillan, 2014), 107.

6. Solnit, op. cit., 71.

7. Quoted in Solnit, op. cit., 42.

8. William Stafford, "At the Un-National Monument along the Canadian Border," *The Way It Is: New & Selected Poems* (St. Paul: Graywolf Press, 1998), 56.

Dialogue (I)

From the PEN Ten Interview with
Randa Jarrar

RANDA JARRAR: When did being a writer begin to inform your sense of identity?

PHILIP METRES: When I was in my teens, I kept getting the sense that certain writers (Eliot, Chekhov, Rilke, Levertov, Dickinson, etc.) and songwriters (Michael Stipe, Paul Westerberg, Bob Mould, Fugazi, etc.) were reading my mind. The unspoken inner life, laid bare on the page, excited and unnerved me. I wanted to access that power. As an introverted young man dealing with the cocktail of hormones surging through my body, I felt as if there were an impossible abyss between myself and others. Writing seemed to stitch together the hurt disjoint between my bodily and psychic experience and my ability to speak through that experience. The idea that I could be a writer gave me great comfort. It was a way to organize and make sense of the anarchy. Writing has always been an oasis for me, a way to step back from certain social flows and pay attention to other, quieter movements (both within and beyond the margins).

What does it mean to be a writer? I think of Henry James's "one upon whom nothing is lost"[1] and Tu Fu's colleague saying "it's like being alive twice."[2] What once seemed like a debility—this self-consciousness, this permeability of self to selves and worlds—when harnessed by language and form, became these flying horses. When I'm not writing for a few days, I feel unmoored, weak-minded, itchy-hearted. Writing is a discipline, a practice, which forms and informs identity.

Joining RAWI (Radius of Arab American Writers) and meeting other Arab American writers allowed me to undergo a certain quantum leap in terms of practicing a writing related to a larger community's dialogue about itself. Though I have always felt welcomed by Arab people, at St. John Melkite Church, for example, it wasn't until I met fellow Arab and Arab American writers that I found brothers and sisters whose worldview was shared, almost without words, and who could coax and challenge each other to become better writers and better denizens of the planet.

RJ: When, if ever, is censorship acceptable?

PM: What is it that we mean by censorship, exactly? Instinctively, I side with Khaled Mattawa—that the question probably is not *when*, but *who*.[3] It might be true that censorship is necessary to limit exposure of certain traumatic or degrading images to children, yet governments do it because they act as if they believe their citizenry to be children. This question also implies a fixed idea about information and its prohibition, texts and the prohibition of texts, images and the prohibition of images—a problem that the West has not had for at least fifty years—except perhaps when it comes to disruptions of the imperial narrative, like the nearly twenty-year prohibition from photographing a flag-draped coffin of an American serviceman killed in the War on Terror or images of dead Iraqis.

Which means, really, that this is a question about how we feel the rest of the world should behave (more like us?). Let's look in the mirror, though. First, we fancy ourselves a free society, and the free flow of information promises to ensure a certain robustness in our democracy. It may well be that the overflow of information, however, functions as a sort of disinformation. The digital age's quantum speed and quantity of available information seem to have a paralyzing effect on us; in the hectic hurtle and voluble volume, the deluge renders the visible unseen, the way a flood obscures a drowning swimmer. There appears almost no time to reflect, to grasp onto something rooted, in the onrush of the present, as we're surrounded by the seethe. It's probably almost unthinkable to the generation of the Free Speech Movement and the Pentagon Papers that the very overflow of information could resemble a form of censorship. Without a robust independent journalistic class, without independent public intellectuals, the deluge of information and disinformation is simply too much for a regular citizen to manage, thus sending him scurrying back into the security of previously held views. The Trump presidency has exacerbated the problem by spurring a crisis in facticity itself, with talk of "fake news" and "alternative facts."

Second, as I mentioned above, there is also de facto censorship in a number of areas of American reportage. However liberal the mass media—and I include National Public Radio and *The New York Times* in this—it still consistently promulgates the imperial narrative, the interests of the ruling class. Under the Bush Administration, more government documents were classified than perhaps ever in history. The Obama administration, which prided itself on transparency, slow-pedaled Freedom of Information Act requests and attacked whistleblowers.

Third, there is also a censorship by limiting access. A number of prominent Arab poets—among them, the Palestinian Ghassan Zaqtan and the Jordanian Amjad Nasser— have been denied visas or so delayed in being granted visas that they've had to cancel speaking tours in the United States. The bureaucratized imperial security state has limited the flow of people who might dare to speak against it. Who knows exactly why they were denied or their process was slowed? But the consequence is chilling. At the same time, Palestinian Americans have been denied entry into Israel, for probably more or less the same reasons. They disrupt the narrative simply by their presence and their witness.

Finally, we have the biggest open secret of all, which is the fact of digital surveillance regimes. Our era may well be known for the digital version of Jeremy Bentham's "perfect" prison, in which all are visible yet are watched by an invisible central authority.[4] The digital traces become a kind of map by which we can be seen, like contrails behind a jet—except these traces attain a strange permanence in an ever-widening digital sky. We are disciplined in ways that we know and do not know, going with the global flows.

So we live in an age in which, paradoxically, everything appears visible and yet much is hidden, perhaps more than ever before. Where we stand, and how our being-in-the-world is related to other beings in the world, how the operations of increasingly complex economic and political systems involve us, seem as obscured as they ever were.

Perhaps the poet's role is to be a reader as much as a writer. To be a reframer of that which already exists. To slow, to disrupt, to interrupt the flows.

RJ: What's the most daring thing you've ever put into words?

PM: If I have to name one instance of daring, I'd say it was in "Homefront," where I wrote, "Sometimes I'm afraid I'm carrying a bomb. That I'm a sleeper and don't know when I'll awaken."[5] Arab Americans don't joke about bombs. Ever. Certainly not over the phone, which we presume is bugged. But this line spoke itself to me, about the secret self-poisoning of Orientalism. You begin to believe what the other says about you and your kind. Read African American literature for one minute and you'll feel the same thing, this attempt to throw off a weight that has been internalized, the weight of hate.

RJ: Where is the line between observation and surveillance?

PM: Both are modes of watching, but who is the watcher, and where does she stand? When I read the Standard Operating Procedure manual of the Guantanamo Bay Prison in the process of writing *Sand Opera*, I was struck by how the United States conceives itself as a country of laws and procedure and regulation. The SOP distinctly demonstrated the level of cultural sensitivity toward the Muslim prisoners that they anticipated would be held there. For example, there were regulations for the proper handling of the Qu'ran, for the call to prayer, and even for Muslim burials. And yet, we know there is an underside of the Law, what Slavoj Žižek has called the Kant/Sade dynamic of Western Enlightenment. We also know that at that same prison, interrogators threw Qu'rans into the toilet in front of prisoners. Female interrogators sexually assaulted prisoners, smearing them with what they thought was menstrual blood. So our sublime cultural sensitivity, our keen cultural awareness became weaponized. Our intelligence became "intelligence." Probably even "cultural awareness" is worthy of scare quotes, given the weird Orientalism that underlays the strategies of "enhanced interrogation." As in: "Arab men don't like to be humiliated by a woman," etc. I don't know many people who like to be humiliated by anyone. And even if they do, they have a safe word.

Surveillance is observation without consequences. It is a power relationship, viewing from afar, without the knowledge of the viewed. The danger of our post-9/11 world is not merely that we know that we are being surveilled; it is that we have willingly acceded the realm of the private in our daily lives. Social media has become another way that we can be controlled. If observation means witness, then it can never be surveillance, because the witness is one who stands in and testifies to their position and the position of the viewed simultaneously. To witness is to stand with oneself and with others, without regard for the consequences.

Notes

1. Henry James, "The Art of Fiction," in *The Theory of Fiction: Henry James*, eds. Henry James and James Edwin Miller (Lincoln: University of Nebraska Press, 1972), 35.

2. John Matthias, "Old Friends and Old Selves," in *Reading Old Friends: Essays, Reviews, and Poems on Poetics 1975–1990* (Albany: State University of New York Press, 1992), 16.

3. Khaled Mattawa, interview by Randa Jarrar, "The PEN Ten with Khaled Mattawa," *PEN America*, June 16, 2015, https://pen.org/the-pen-ten-with-khaled-mattawa/

4. Jeremy Bentham, *The Works of Jeremy Bentham, Now First Collected* (Ann Arbor: University of Michigan, 1838).

5. Philip Metres, "Homefront / Removes: A Narrative of the Renditions of Mohamad Farag Ahmad Bashmilah," in *Sand Opera* (Farmington: Alice James, 2015), 93.

Essays & Portraits (I)

Beyond Grief and Grievance

American Poetry in the Wake of 9/11

(2011)

It was the Tuesday of my second week as a newly minted professor in the Midwest, and I hustled to complete a lecture on imagery in poems, when my wife called. All I could think was "why is she calling me ten minutes before I have to teach?"—something about a plane crash something something New York—and then "why do I need to know this before class?" September 11, 2001.

I hung up, and returned to the poem before me, Carolyn Forché's "The Colonel."

By the time I arrived in the classroom, after hearing the full extent of the morning's events, I could barely get through the poem without breaking into tears.

It's not just the bag of ears that the Colonel pours across his opulent table, in a gesture of shock and awe. It's the violence at the perimeters of vision—the filed nails of the daughter, the moon hanging on a cord, the house surrounded by a wall of broken bottles, the gratings on the window, even the rack of lamb.

The poem works not merely by intimating torture, but by decorating it so uncannily like the homes of privilege in our own country. In the Colonel's home, an American cop show blares on the television, and a maid serves a dinner worthy of a Robert Hass poem—in short, bourgeois comfort and plenty. Forché's poem, in its raw confrontation, jolts us awake to the violence of privilege. But that's what made it so difficult to teach on that day. What was 9/11 but the end of the fantasy of our separateness, our invulnerability?

Poetry—and the poetic mode of elegy—emerged as a popular response to the terrorist attacks of September 11, 2001, often

17

bringing succor, complicating grief, and embodying grievance. The events of 9/11 occasioned a tremendous outpouring of poetry; in New York, poems were taped on windows, wheatpasted on posts, shared by hand. In Curtis Fox's words, "poetry was suddenly everywhere in the city."[1]

Aided by email, listservs, websites, and blogs, thousands of people shared poetry. By February 2002, over 25,000 poems in response to 9/11 had been published on one amateur poetry site. Three years later, the number of poems had more than doubled. Though those poems disappeared along with the website, they served many purposes, not least among them was to attempt to make some sense out of the radically insensible trauma of that day. Some, certainly, employed the language of faith, a faith that has often been mobilized as a weapon of grievance. Some were desperately angry, in the way Toby Keith's "Courtesy of the Red, White, and Blue (The Angry American)" promises to put a "boot in the ass" of those that "messed" with the United States. In Cleveland, I recall hearing some salty Osama limericks involving his mama. We don't know how long we'll live, nor whether our words will outlast us. But poems are not just built for eternity. They are the argot of our everyday life, and sometimes we jury-rig them, with outworn rhymes and ossified clichés, to make it possible to live.

Into all this lyrical democracy, Ezra Pound (by way of *ABC of Reading*) pokes in his arrogant head to remind us that "Good writers are those that keep the language efficient. That is to say, keep it accurate, keep it clear."[2] And "a people that grows accustomed to sloppy writing is a people in process of losing grip on its empire and on itself. And this looseness and blowsiness is not anything as simple and scandalous as abrupt and disordered syntax."[3] Sloppy writing, sloppy thinking, sloppy empire; sounds like the recipe for the invasion of Iraq.

The truth is that good poems are always linguistic occasions in themselves. Poems that take on subjects as iconic as the attacks of September 11th risk not only devolving into cliché but also perpetuating the violence of terror and the violence of grievance and revenge, as mass media did by endlessly replaying images of the planes exploding into the World Trade Center

18

towers. One of the worst films about 9/11, to my mind, is "United 93"; for all its devotion to facticity, it does not add one iota of insight. On the contrary, it begins in the most clichéd (and anti-Muslim) way possible, with the sounds of Arabic prayers murmured by the terrorists; a far more provocative beginning would have been at the strip clubs and porn shops these supposedly devout men had frequented prior to the attacks.

Likewise, when we read enough 9/11 poems, we become awash in falling people, planes described as birds, flaming towers of Babel, ash and angels, angels and ash. The mythic character of this attack, this disaster—bringing to mind the tower of Babel and the fall of Icarus—is undeniable, and the acts of heroism and the brute loss of so many makes it difficult to find adequate words. In his most poetic moment, New York mayor Rudolph Giuliani, when asked how many had died, replied, "more than we can bear."[4]

Polish poet Wislawa Szymborska meditates on one such iconic image in her poem, "Photograph from September 11":

They jumped from the burning floors—
one, two, a few more,
higher, lower.

The photograph halted them in life,
and now keeps them
above the earth toward the earth.

Each is still complete,
with a particular face
and blood well hidden.

There's enough time
for hair to come loose,
for keys and coins
to fall from pockets.

They're still within the air's reach,
within the compass of places
that have just now opened.

I can do only two things for them—
describe this flight
and not add a last line.[5]

Here, Szymborska takes the photograph of the so-called "falling man," the trigger to a number of poems and at least two novels (Don DeLillo's *The Falling Man* and Jonathan Safran Foer's *Extremely Loud and Incredibly Close*). Yet, in our light touch, she makes what could become cliché into a monument of our elegiac desire to freeze the beloved in the moments before death, to see the beloved in flight, where they are still "within . . . reach." Still, somehow, the poem stays within the bounds of acceptable grief.

Walt Whitman once lamented, "the real war will never get in the books."[6] Trauma evades language; cataclysmic events don't settle easily on the page. Perhaps even more troubling than the possibility of art's perpetuation of violence is its exploitation for easy (and false) transcendence. In a riposte to a commemorative essay, "Remembering 9/11 through Poetry," one commenter acidly posted: "isn't 9/11 bad enough without adding poetry to it?"

The commenter may just be a poetry-hater, but he also has a point, made more articulately by Theodor Adorno, that "to write lyric poetry after Auschwitz is barbaric."[7] Adorno reflects on the dangers of art to render traumatic events too easily understandable, too easily commodifiable. In his essay, "Commitment," Adorno extends his original critique, saying that

> by turning suffering into images, harsh and uncompromising though they are, it wounds the shame we feel in the presence of the victims. For these victims are used to create something, works of art, that are thrown to the consumption of a world which destroyed them. . . . The moral of this art, not to forget for a single instant, slithers into the abyss of its opposite. The aesthetic principle of stylization, and even the solemn prayer of the chorus, make an unthinkable fate appear to have had some meaning; it is transfigured, something of its horror removed. This alone does an injustice to the victims; yet no art which tried to evade them could confront the claims of justice.[8]

With such pressure to avoid doing injustice to the victims, it is no wonder that it has become commonplace to say that the best poem about 9/11 is W. H. Auden's "September 1st, 1939," a poem written to mark the German invasion of Poland, a poem Auden would expurgate from his *Collected Poems,* for its clichéd concluding stanzas. It was certainly among the most circulated poems after the attacks, and among the most discussed, though this poem's relevance to the events, and its position as the best 9/11 poem, is questionable at best. Saying otherwise is to wash one's hands of reading how contemporary poets tried to bring language to bear this particular unbearability.

One could also say, for example, that the most important work of art to emerge from the Iraq War was the blue curtain, hung to cover Picasso's "Guernica" at the entrance of the Security Council in the United Nations, before which Secretary of State Colin Powell would argue that Iraq was an imminent threat, and that war was necessary. One could say the same about the digital photos taken at the Abu Ghraib prison.

But we cannot be silent. So between the Scylla of cliché and the Charybdis of exploitation, poetry moves. In an interview on the day of the attacks, Billy Collins proposed that "you could pick any poem, almost from any book, and that poem would be against what happened today," and later suggested that "one could do worse than reading one of the Psalms today."[9] Yet he later wrote "The Names," when he was asked by the Librarian of Congress to write a poem for the one-year anniversary in 2002. In contrast to "The Names," the 9/11 poems that will last may well be the ones that either subvert 9/11 clichés or explore new voices that deconstruct the easy ahistorical and nationalist narrative of the attack, poems like Martín Espada's "Alabanza: In Praise of Local 100," Michael Magee's "Political Song, Confused Voicing," and Mohja Kahf's "My Grandmother Washes Her Feet in the Sink of the Bathroom at Sears."

Martín Espada's "Alabanza: In Praise of Local 100"—*alabanza* means "praise"—offers a globalist ode to the workers on the restaurant at the top of the World Trade Center who perished in the attacks. By focusing on people unnoticed or disparaged, Espada celebrates the diverse gathering of humanity that the American project has enabled, and that the attacks threatened to separate, in the rhetoric of security and the ideology of fear. The poem begins:

> *Alabanza.* Praise the cook with a shaven head
> and a tattoo on his shoulder that said Oye,
> a blue-eyed Puerto Rican with people from Fajardo,
> the harbor of pirates centuries ago.
> Praise the lighthouse in Fajardo, candle
> glimmering white to worship the dark saint of the sea.
> *Alabanza.* Praise the cook's yellow Pirates cap
> worn in the name of Roberto Clemente, his plane
> that flamed into the ocean loaded with cans for Nicaragua,
> for all the mouths chewing the ash of earthquakes.
> *Alabanza.* Praise the kitchen radio, dial clicked
> even before the dial on the oven, so that music and Spanish
> rose before bread. Praise the bread. *Alabanza.*[10]

The poem's concluding lines brings the victims of war—from the 9/11 victims to the victims of war in Afghanistan—into conversation again:

> *Alabanza.* When the war began, from Manhattan and Kabul
> two constellations of smoke rose and drifted to each other,
> mingling in icy air, and one said with an Afghan tongue:
> *Teach me to dance. We have no music here.*
> And the other said with a Spanish tongue:
> *I will teach you. Music is all we have.*[11]

Perhaps the best response to Adorno's legitimate concerns is that "music is all we have."

It would be strange to talk about poetry and 9/11 and not mention Amiri Baraka's scandal-making and splenetic "Somebody Blew Up America," published in 2002. At the time, Baraka held the post of New Jersey's poet laureate, and his poem caused an outcry, principally for perpetuating an Internet myth that 4,000 Israelis vacated the Twin Towers prior to their destruction, and secondarily for its anti-imperialist rant against the United States and the Bush Administration. His subsequent defense of the poem, an essay called "I Will Not 'Apologize,' I Will Not 'Resign,'" did not do the work any favors; rather than arguing that the poem is the dramatized utterance of a suppressed but necessary point of view—that of the anti-imperialist scourge—Baraka asserts his absolute identification with the poem's rhetoric.[12]

The poem may be smarter than the poet's argument on its behalf. Emerging from an event that has ignited as many conspiracy theories as JFK's assassination, "Somebody Blew Up America" enacts the intoxification of conspiracy-theorizing itself. Conspiracy theory, spastic groping after fact and reason, comes out of the fantasy of absolute governmental power. While the poem's catalogue of imperial atrocity is mostly documentable (with the glaring exception being Israeli and American administration complicity in the attacks), the desire to place all the blame on a singular "Somebody" dramatizes the weakness of a totalizing critique of empire.

The ending of the poem clinches this reading: "Who and Who and WHO (+) who who/Whoooo and WhooooOOOOOOooooOooo!"[13] The poem's comic-gothic, loony-bird ending actually suggests the dangers of the slippery thinking of conspiracy theories, even as it relishes in it. With that final stretched "who," it's as if the wise bird is more interested in the sound of its own voice, its own conspiracy-theory echo chamber.

Emerging from the Flarf Collective—Flarf itself being very much a post-9/11 poetry—Mike Magee's "Political Song, Confused Voicing" activates the politics and poetics of grievance. The poem blisters with energetic and absurdist wordplay; it begins:

> you tongued my battleship!
> you bonged my tattle-tale!
> you maimed my mamby-pamby
> Wagnered my Nietzsche
> and gotcha'd my sweatshop
>
> there ain't room in heaven for us[14]

In short, you [blanked] me! This structure suggests a feeling of grievance or woundedness, but the poet flings so many allusions at us—from commercials to board games to political acronyms to philosophy—that we are suspended in its comic-furious catalogue. The first line, "you tongued my battleship" both references the commercial for the game "Battleship"—in which the boy says to his sister, "you sunk my battleship!"—and the bombing of the U.S.S. *Cole* in 2001, dramatizing American subjectivity's collage of history and games, and war itself as a commodity.

But the poem gains pathos and power with its blues refrain, and confuses any simplistic reading of who is the "us" and who is the "them." Is the "us" of the refrain, who have no room in heaven, the terrorists, or the Americans who appear to be speaking the main stanzas? The poem ends:

you prayed on my carpet
you bombed my parade

and there ain't room in heaven
no there ain't room in heaven
no there ain't room in heaven for us[15]

The voices get confused in ways that suggest that the "us" is the wider human race, since "you prayed on my carpet" could be the typical complaint of bin Laden about American military presence in Saudi Arabia, and "you bombed my parade" could refer either to the U.S. economic parade ending or the U.S. bombings of wedding parties in Afghanistan or Iraq. Grievances wind together in ways that suggest that competing grievances become a vicious circle, collapsing the distance between us and the terrorists. Magee employs the power of grievance even as the poem distrusts its consequences.

The New Yorker published a number of often-moving poems, including Adam Zagajewski's "Try to Praise the Mutilated World," W. S. Merwin's "To the Words," Deborah Garrison's "I Saw You Walking," C. K. Williams' "War," and Galway Kinnell's "When the Towers Fell." In particular, though at the time I thought "Try to Praise the Mutilated World" was too plain, too straight to be commensurate with the radical derangement of the attacks, I now see it as a poem whose quietness is a stay against the confusion of those days. Though "Try to Praise" was written prior to the attacks, it was prescient and wise. I could have used more lines like: "you've seen the refugees heading nowhere, / you've heard the executioners sing joyfully. / You should praise the mutilated world. / Remember the moments when we were together / in a white room and the curtain fluttered."[16]

I could also mention Bob Hicok's ruminative "Full Flight," Frank Bidart's nail-slamming "The Curse," Ann Lauterbach's incantatory "Hum," Robyn Schiff's gyring "Project Paperclip," and a host of other poets and poems—both about 9/11 and those written earlier that we read differently after 9/11 (for example, Thomas Lux's Gulf War-era "The People of the Other Village"). H. L. Hix's brilliant docupoetic *God Bless*—which deploys the language used by Bush and bin Laden to create a formally complex and provocative dialogue in verse—deserves a central place in the canon of 9/11 poetry.

Who didn't try writing a poem about 9/11? One poet-friend, whom I admire for his independence, pronounced his utter disinterest in the subject. I respect his sense that poetry could not go there without losing itself. For me, and for other Arab Americans, it was impossible not to write about and through the 9/11 attacks. Perhaps every poem I've written since 9/11 is inflected, in some way, by 9/11.

It's also difficult, in many respects, to separate 9/11 from the subsequent war in Afghanistan, the imperial adventure in Iraq, and even the economic meltdown. Yet poems by Arab American poets such as Suheir Hammad's "First Writing Since," Naomi Shihab Nye's "Letter to any Would-Be Terrorists," Sam Hazo's "September 11, 2001," Lawrence Joseph's "Inclined to Speak"— among many others—crystallized the shame and grief and anger of what it meant to live in the gap between Arab and American worlds during those terrifying days since 2001. And more than that: it made some of us feel that we were not alone, that this terrible event came from terror and could lead to terror, and that the witness of poetry was more necessary than ever.

Mohja Kahf's "My Grandmother Washes Her Feet in the Sink of the Bathroom at Sears" comically and thoughtfully invites us all into the same bathroom together: Arab and American, Muslim and non-Muslim, patriarchal and feminist. When her grandmother gets dirty looks, she

catches their meaning and her look in the mirror says,
I have washed my feet over Iznik tile in Istanbul
with water from the world's ancient irrigation systems
I have washed my feet in the bathhouses of Damascus
over painted bowls imported from China
among the best families of Aleppo
And if you Americans knew anything
about civilization and cleanliness,
you'd make wider washbins, anyway
My grandmother knows one culture—the right one,

as do these matrons of the Middle West . . .[17]

Kahf employs gentle comedy as she translates between the world-view of her grandmother and the worldview of "these matrons of the Middle West," holding the door for everyone (literally and figuratively) when they leave the bathroom.

Finally, I'd be remiss if I didn't mention two significant anthologies. *September 11, 2001: American Writers Respond* (Etruscan Books, 2002) gathered poetry and reflections by poets and writers, offering an almost immediate but complex response to the attacks; the poems and letters to the editor William Heyen range from the reflective to the angry, from grief to grievance, from reactionary to radical. Another anthology, *Poetry after 9/11* (Melville House, 2011), has been updated and republished. There is more than enough to read, to read to remember, and to imagine other futures.

The terrorist attacks of September 11, 2001, compelled me to rethink everything I thought I knew and made me want to learn more, to read outside whatever borders I had created for myself. Not to be more American, but to be a better citizen, a better denizen of the planet. To go global and be local, to go ancient and be modern, to question all certainties and embrace what I did not know, to read Rumi and Isaiah, Rushdie and Roy and even Al-Qaeda, to listen to Springsteen and Kulthum, to refuse the elixir of fundamentalisms, to translate and be translated again by what I could not yet understand. To tattoo *Oye* on my body. To listen.

1. Curtis Fox, Poetry Off the Shelf podcast. Date unknown.

2. Ezra Pound, "Chapter Three," in *ABC of Reading* (New York: New Directions, 1934), 32.

3. Ibid., 34.

4. Martha T. Moore, "Giuliani Exudes Toughness but Can Rankle," *ABC News* (New York, NY), January 3, 2008.

5. Wisława Szymborska, "Photograph from September 11," in *Monologue of a Dog*, trans. Clare Cavanagh and Stanisław Barańczak (New York: Harcourt, 2002), 69.

6. Walt Whitman, "The Real War Will Never Get in the Books," in *Specimen Days & Collect* (Philadelphia: David McKay, 1882), 80.

7. Theodor Adorno, "Cultural Criticisms and Society," in *Prisms*, trans. Samuel and Shierry Weber (Cambridge: Massachusetts Institute of Technology Press, 1981), 28.

8. Theodor Adorno, "Commitment," in *Aesthetics and Politics*, trans. Ronald Taylor (New York: Verso, 2002), 189.

9. Peter Kenyon et al., "Apparent Terrorist Attacks on World Trade Center, Pentagon, and Southwestern Pennsylvania," *National Public Radio*, September 11, 2001.

10. Martín Espada, "Alabanza: In Praise of Local 100," in *Alabanza: New and Selected Poems 1982–2002* (New York: W. W. Norton, 2003), 231.

11. Ibid.

12. Amiri Baraka, "I Will Not 'Apologize,' I Will Not 'Resign,'" in *ChickenBones: A Journal for Literary and Artistic African American Themes*, October 2, 2008, www.nathanielturner.com/barakaonwhoblewupamerica.html

13. Amiri Baraka, *Somebody Blew Up America* (Baraka, 2001), 12.

14. Michael Magee, "Political Song, Confused Voicing," in *MS* (New York: Spuyten Duyvil, 2003).

15. Ibid.

16. Adam Zagajewski, "Try to Praise the Mutilated World," *The New Yorker*, September 15, 2003, http://www.newyorker.com/magazine/2003/09/15/september-poems

17. Mohja Kahf, "My Grandmother Washes Her Feet in the Sink of the Bathroom at Sears," in *E-mails from Scheherazad* (Gainesville: University Press of Florida, 2003).

"The School among the Ruins"

Reading Adrienne Rich on a Greyhound Bus

Over twenty years ago, on a Greyhound bus from Bloomington, Indiana, heading home to Chicago—surrounded by the weary and hungover, the longing and the spent, those hurting quietly and those whose eyes won't alight on anything—I opened to the first page of Adrienne Rich's *What Is Found There: Notebooks on Poetry and Politics* (1993): "I saw an atrophy of our power to imagine other ways of navigating into a collective future."[1]

I was sitting next to a man bent double by a stomachache, his breath recalling onions, his clothes soured over days in some private hell. Across the way, urinous light washed the wrinkled page that a tired teen, tapping her teeth with a pen, tried to complete. Somewhere, a cashed-out teen's headphones emitted a muted screech, like furious mice inside a wall. All of us locked away, in the cells of our narrowed selves.

We suffer at the hands of the god of the free market, the god of radical individualism, who tells us we're alone, destined to be lonely. We need each other, and we need to be able to see what binds us. For Rich, poetry could be a way to illuminate our connections, that it could "break open locked chambers of possibility, restore numbed zones to feeling, recharge desire."[2] Opening any of her books was to be opened, and I was lucky to be carrying a stack of them, preparing for my dissertation exams, wrestling with their angels.

On that bus ride in the dark heartland, I lingered over "North American Time" (1983). It begins paradoxically:

When my dreams showed signs
of becoming

        politically correct
        no unruly images
        escaping beyond borders
        when walking in the street I found my
        themes cut out for me
        knew what I would not report
        for fear of enemies' usage
        then I began to wonder[3]

Though Rich prided herself on writing a poetry of political engagement, and exhorted us to political poetry, she also refused
the dangers of becoming "politically correct," slipping too comfortably inside any orthodoxy, whether of the mainstream or the
Democratic Party or the farther Left. She likely was referring
specifically to the "correctness" of the period, not the "P.C." derided by the Right since the late 1980s. Her life and her poetry,
after all, called her to connections with those who had been left
out of the networks of power, and that the powerful would always try to co-opt that language or hold it against the poet:

        Everything we write
        will be used against us
        or against those we love.
        These are the terms,
        take them or leave them.
        Poetry never stood a chance
        of standing outside history.
        One line typed twenty years ago
        can be blazed on a wall in spraypaint
        glorify art as detachment
        or torture of those we
        did not love but also
        did not want to kill

        We move but our words stand
        become responsible
        far more than we intended

        and this is verbal privilege[4]

Rich knows that poetry is a devil's bargain. Her brilliant en-jambment, "Poetry never stood a chance / of standing outside history," embodies the "forced choice" of the artist living in em-pire: either our language goes unheard or it is summoned into networks of power, which constantly misquote us or bend our words to other meanings or deracinate them, tear them from their (and our) attachments.

It is why Rich would come to refuse the National Medal for the Arts in 1997 (the only person ever to do so), saying, "I could not accept such an award from President Clinton or this White House because the very meaning of art, as I understand it, is in-compatible with the cynical politics of this administration."[5] And later, when she wrote to clarify her position, she added: "There is no simple formula for the relationship of art to justice. But I do know that art—in my own case the art of poetry—means nothing if it simply decorates the dinner table of power which holds it hostage."[6]

"North American Time" locates the poet in the vexing ques-tions that she, as a North American poet, must face—that even if she has the chance to speak, the terrible oppression of people may not be mitigated by her words. Further, that her very words may be used against her and those she loves. And finally, that what she must sit down to and contemplate "is meant to break my heart and reduce me to silence."[7] Between the grief of the ancestors of the enslaved, and the shame of the ancestors of the enslavers, by the end of the poem, Rich, the North American poet, "starts to speak again."[8] Rich kept writing, refusing the blinkering benefits of the privilege she was born to.

At the same time that she would refuse to accept the blessings of the powerful, she resisted the easy seductions of propagan-distic art. In *What Is Found There*, on that bus, I read: "You could derive from Trotsky's assertion, that an 'engaged' or 'commit-ted' art, an art critical of society, the kind of art usually labeled 'political' in the United States, is bad (when it is bad) not be-cause it is engaged, but because *it is not engaged enough*; when it tries to express what has been logically understood but not yet organically assimilated."[9]

Reading them on that bus, the words struck me with force. I'd been researching the 1991 Gulf War and the poetic responses to it, and finding many of the poems uninspired, topical, and obvious. The war had been my unholy baptism into the realities of American empire. In the fall of 1990, after the invasion of Kuwait by Iraq, the cries for war rose in Washington; in what was my first public political gesture, I organized a rally at my quiet college on the hill to call for a nonmilitary solution. It was thrilling to see so many people on the library steps, listening to one speaker after another make impassioned and articulate arguments for restraint and against empire. *No Blood for Oil*, our signs read, as we circled the sidewalk.

But what I remember most was, in the arctic cold of January, being outside, watching my classmates inside huddled around the common room television, their bodies leaning in with excitement. I must have been inside at first, but probably I couldn't stand it. When war was declared, their thrilled voices punctured the air, reaching me beyond the windows. The dark night sky of Baghdad—which looked green because of night vision filters—filled with tracer fire and rocked with explosions. The war, thoroughly censored from the beginning, was depicted as a clean war, a chance for America to regain its confidence after the "Vietnam syndrome." I thought my country had gone crazy. The child of a Vietnam veteran, the son of an Arab American, I knew in my bones that beneath that ardor and awe of our own might were the cries of those we could not hear, who would be disappeared twice: first by weapons, then by our representation of that war.

I left the country for Russia, wanting to see how other poets dealt with their own political oppression. In the years that followed, I tried to read everything I could about that war, to make sense of it again, and to learn what poets did to try to stop it from happening again. I hungered for words and forms that could oppose an empire's might.

The wisdom of Rich's words about a truly political poetry rang true, given the failures of the poems I'd read responding to the Gulf War. To find and write a poetry that has organically assimilated its politics, that knows what it knows in the bones, has attained a kind of talismanic mystery that I'm still learning twenty years later. Some of the greatest lyric political poets—Akhmatova, Rukeyser, Lowell, Neruda, Brooks, Rich, Darwish—

testify to a vision not reducible to headlines, momentary protest, or harangue. And while she kept a space open for topical work, what drew her own mind and ignited her imagination was the life of the collective, all its pockets and margins, where people go mute, are broken, or disappear. She refused the resignation of the privileged, who call poetry an art for specialists, for the elite, for aesthetes. She wanted poetry to be larger than itself, as the Russian literary tradition has it: "a poet in Russia is more than a poet."

In 1974, upon winning the National Book Award for *Diving into the Wreck*, Rich delivered an address that she and two other finalists cowrote:

> We, Audre Lorde, Adrienne Rich, and Alice Walker, together accept this award in the name of all the women whose voices have gone and still go unheard in a patriarchal world, and in the name of those who, like us, have been tolerated as token women in this culture, often at great cost and in great pain. We believe that we can enrich ourselves more in supporting and giving to each other than by competing against each other; and that poetry—if it is poetry—exists in a realm beyond ranking and comparison. We symbolically join together here in refusing the terms of patriarchal competition and declaring that we will share this prize among us, to be used as best we can for women. We appreciate the good faith of the judges for this award, but none of us could accept this money for herself, nor could she let go unquestioned the terms on which poets are given or denied honor and livelihood in this world, especially when they are women. We dedicate this occasion to the struggle for self-determination of all women, of every color, identification, or derived class: the poet, the housewife, the lesbian, the mathematician, the mother, the dishwasher, the pregnant teenager, the teacher, the grandmother, the prostitute, the philosopher, the waitress, the women who will understand what we are doing here and those who will not understand yet; the silent women whose voice have been denied us, the articulate women who have given us strength to do our work.[10]

The gesture she made with Lorde and Walker was more than symbolic; it was the quintessence of her poetic practice, both intimately personal and powerfully collective. It drew together a collective of women, many of whom would never encounter a poem by Rich or Lorde or Walker, but whose struggles were held and regarded as part of a larger work of liberation and self-determination.

She could not bear everyone's burden, but she wanted to behold them in her mind as she wrote, and taught, and advocated, to write them closer together. On that bus, reading "An Atlas of the Difficult World" (1991), I found the sort of poetry that moved beyond topical response to the Gulf War, suturing together dislocated lives and fates across the country, burned by predatory capitalism, racism, and war. "Atlas" (1991) returns to the concerns of "North American Time," engaging in an imaginative mapping project of the nation, drawing together diverse subjectivities and locations. Beginning with a "dark woman, head bent, listening for something"[11]—which could be the migrant farm worker picking strawberries in the fields that appears shortly thereafter—the poem ranges in time and space, from voice to voice attempting to suture the painful distances that isolate and pull us apart. In the first section, the range of people and chorus of voices augur what is to come in the poem; from the mute worker to the aesthete who notices the pond's light is "finer than my mother's handkerchief / received from her mother, hemmed and initialed / by the nuns in Belgium."[12] The voices run against each other without comment, as if marking their isolation, suddenly sutured in the poem. From Annie Sullivan's memories of an Irish workhouse to George Jackson's reflections on Soledad Prison, from witnessing a spider weaving a web between the poet's candlesticks to observations about the ubiquitous girasol (sunflower), from imaginations of a suicide to the story of a lesbian couple murdered in the hills, Rich's poem tries to make sense of this wrecked and beautiful country.

In Section XI, Rich gets explicit about her desire to create a map of this troubled country, trying to recuperate the idea of the poet patriot—not as an abettor of empire, but as a prophetic voice of conscience, who marched against the Gulf War alongside

. . . some for whom war is new, others for whom it merely
    continues the old paroxysms of time
some marching for peace who for twenty years did not
    march for justice
some for whom peace is a white man's word and a white
    man's privilege
some who have learned to handle and contemplate the
    shapes of powerlessness and power
as the nurse learns hip and thigh and weight of the body he
    has to lift and sponge, day upon day
as she blows with her every skill on the spirit's embers still
    burning by their own laws in the bed of death.
A patriot is not a weapon. A patriot is one who wrestles for
    the soul of her country
as she wrestles for her own being, for the soul of his country
(gazing through the great circle at Window Rock into the
    sheen of the Viet Nam Wall)
as he wrestles for his own being. A patriot is a citizen trying
    to wake
from the burnt-out dream of innocence, the nightmare
of the white general and the Black general posed in their
    camouflage,
to remember her true country, remember his suffering land:
    remember
that blessing and cursing are born as twins and separated at
    birth to meet again in mourning
that the internal emigrant is the most homesick of all women
    and of all men
that every flag that flies today is a cry of pain.[13]

Rich catalogs the demonstrators, who might oppose the war
but also hide their own complicities and forsake a difficult patriotism, one that acknowledges our connection to place and
to each other. In discussing a war where the Patriot missile—a
guided missile that was alleged falsely to be highly successful in
eliminating Iraq's SCUD missiles—was called the first hero of
the war, according to CNN, Rich sees the patriot as "one who
wrestles for the soul of her country." The false patriotism of
ticker-tape triumphalism was in abundance during the Gulf War.
But Rich does not focus on the outrageously whitewashed narrative of that war. Instead, she sees in all those flags "a cry of

pain." She knows that patriotism is a refuge to those who have sacrificed their lives for their country and those whose lives are full of suffering.

In a poem filled with the solitary and broken, the paradoxical "loneliness together" of "Atlas" drives its beautiful Whitmanic conclusion, inviting us—all of us atomized in our own loneliness and despair, echoing her National Book Award statement with Lorde and Walker—into the space of the beloved:

> I know you are reading this poem in a waiting-room
> of eyes met and unmeeting, of identity with strangers.
> I know you are reading this poem by fluorescent light
> in the boredom and fatigue of the young who are counted
> out,
> count themselves out, at too early an age.
> . . .
> I know you are reading this poem listening for something,
> torn
> between bitterness and hope
> turning back once again to the task you cannot refuse.
> I know you are reading this poem because there is nothing
> else
> left to read
> there where you have landed, stripped as you are.[14]

In this litany of alienated subjectivities, Rich sits with us in the moment of reading, wherever we've landed (all of us, in some respect, are aliens landing).

On that bus ride, in the dark, we passed so many struggling towns, invisible except for a few house lights. So many places in this country plundered by neoliberalism, by globalization, all of it carved for profit. Rich would write about a wild place in "What Kind of Times Are These" that had not yet been sold off, "a place between two stands of trees" that she refuses to map for the reader.[15] It was a place where "the persecuted / who disappeared into those shadows" still linger in the mind.[16] Rich's poetry was in that place, not to exploit the shadows for her own gain but to listen to its lost voices, to mark the place of disappearance. What's remarkable about the poem is her refusal to tell us, her readers, where it is, to honor it by not using it:

> I won't tell you where the place is, the dark mesh of the
>   woods
> meeting the unmarked strip of light—
> ghost-ridden crossroads, leafmold paradise:
> I know already who wants to buy it, sell it, make it disappear.
>
> And I won't tell you where it is, so why do I tell you
> anything? Because you still listen, because in times like these
> to have you listen at all, it's necessary
> to talk about trees.[17]

What I love about the odd ending is how it wrestles with her readers who hunger only for a poetry about nature, of birds and trees. At the same time, the poem argues with one of the great political writers, Bertolt Brecht. Brecht famously wrote "you can't write poems about trees when the woods are full of policemen," and in his poem, "To Those Who Follow in My Wake": "What times are these, in which / A conversation about trees is almost a crime / For in doing so we maintain our silence about so much wrongdoing!"[18] If Brecht was protesting against a detached and aestheticized "nature" poetry, Rich ironically recuperates it as an image first of enticement (dear poetry reader, all you care about is trees, so here are your trees!), and then as an image of what we can never destroy without destroying ourselves.

When the terrorist attacks of September 11th happened, Rich had already written the poem that would become the title to her book written during those years: "The School among the Ruins." It became a prophecy of 9/11. In contrast to the massively grotesque spectacle of 9/11, Rich's poem quietly turned its attentive gaze toward all the other places in the world—which the epigraph lists as "Beirut. Baghdad. Sarajevo. Bethlehem. Kabul. Not of course here."—where people are imperiled.[19]

In the poignant fourth section, Rich takes on the voice of the teacher in this school among the ruins:

> One: I don't know where your mother
> is Two: I don't know
> why they are trying to hurt us
> Three: or the latitude and longitude
> of their hatred Four: I don't know if we

hate them as much I think there's more toilet paper
in the supply closet I'm going to break it open
Today this is your lesson:
write as clearly as you can
your name home street and number
down on this page
No you can't go home yet
but you aren't lost
this is our school[20]

Rich's poem brings to light the daily struggle of teachers everywhere, working with children living in violence and under oppression, trying to deal with lack of supplies, doing the basic
work of helping them to learn to write their own names, and
where they come from. Rich's poems, for me, were their own
education, about how to write with my ear and mouth directed
toward the shadows, the margins, where so many have been disappeared.

Back on the bus, my suffering seatmate departed, and in his
stead, Gloria, a vivacious twentysomething black woman. In
the age before cell phones, it was easier to reach each other,
so it didn't take me long to learn where she was going and why.
Months before, she'd been relocated from her apartment in the
Robert Taylor housing project to Columbus, and was now going back to do some Christmas shopping and see family and
friends. She was thrilled to be going home, even though it was
no longer where she lived, even though her old building and
community (ruptured as it may have been) no longer existed.
Sitting and talking with Gloria, the miles and hours melted away,
in the thrall sharing stories, her life, my life. We only grew quiet
as we began to near the lights of the city.

Rich will be justly remembered for her groundbreaking essays on motherhood, women's literature, and queer liberation;
for her love poetry as well as her political verse; for her early
seething urn-like formalism and her wide-ranging and speculative mature verse; for her principled stands against oppression,
refusing prizes and honors given by organizations and governments who committed injustices; for reminding us of Rukeyser
and bringing so many other lost or unheard women's voices to

our attention. I remember her for how she always called us to the root (a word she loved), to recognize our deep and often unseen connections, to ourselves, to each other, to the planet.

A decade ago, when I read the news that Rich died, I didn't feel grief. Was it because I never knew her except through her words, which will not die? What a vibrating, pulsing voice in the words Rich left behind—a light to find ourselves by, as that frozen night we rode the bus, heading to the places we still called home, though they only existed in our minds. Stripped as we are.

Notes

1. Adrienne Rich, "Preface," in *What Is Found There: Notebooks on Poetry and Politics* (New York: W. W. Norton, 1993), xiii.

2. Ibid., xiv.

3. Adrienne Rich, "North American Time," in *Your Native Land, Your Life* (New York: W. W. Norton, 1986).

4. Ibid.

5. Adrienne Rich, "Why I Refused the National Medal for the Arts," in *Arts of the Possible: Essays and Conversations* (New York: W. W. Norton, 2001).

6. Ibid.

7. Adrienne Rich, "North American Time."

8. Ibid.

9. Adrienne Rich, "The Muralist," in *What Is Found There: Notebooks on Poetry and Politics* (New York: W. W. Norton, 1993), 46–47.

10. Adrienne Rich, acceptance speech, 1974 National Book Award, quoted in Claudia Rankine, introduction to *Collected Poems: 1950–2012*, by Adrienne Rich (New York: W. W. Norton, 2016).

11. Adrienne Rich, "An Atlas of the Difficult World," in *An Atlas of the Difficult World: Poems 1988–1991* (New York: W. W. Norton, 1991), 3.

12. Ibid.

13. Ibid., 23.

14. Ibid., 25–26.

15. Adrienne Rich, "What Kind of Times Are These," in *Dark Fields of the Republic: Poems 1991–1995* (New York: W. W. Norton, 1995), 1.

16. Ibid.

17. Ibid.

18. Bertolt Brecht, "To Those Who Follow in Our Wake," in *Svenberg's*

(1939), in *Collected Works* (1967), vol. 4, 222–25, quoted in Scott Horton, "To Those Who Follow in Our Wake," trans. Scott Horton, *Harper's Magazine,* January 15, 2008, http://harpers.org/blog/2008/01/brecht-to-those-who-follow-in-our-wake/

19. Adrienne Rich, "The School among the Ruins," in *The School Among the Ruins: Poems 2000–2004* (New York: W. W. Norton, 2004), 22.

20. Ibid., 24.

Carrying Continents in Our Eyes
Arab American Poetry after 9/11

"You look just like that terrorist from *United 93*," my Arab American father said, laughing at the resemblance. He'd just seen the movie about the hijacking of the plane that went down in Shanksville, Pennsylvania, thanks to the heroism of passengers who learned that the flight was likely to be the third plane of the 9/11 attacks.

My always-direct father was right. It was spooky to see actor Khalid Abdulla on-screen, like the version of myself that had been born in the Middle East, attempt to take down a plane and murder thousands. That recognition is all too familiar to Arab Americans, who for most of our history in America have found ourselves cast only as villains, whether in movies or on the news. *Denial*, my dad loves to say, *is not just a river in Egypt*.

Neither a Muslim nor a member of al-Qaeda, a third-generation Arab American, I nevertheless found myself in the weeks following the attacks on a university panel called "Making Sense of September 11th," articulating the laundry list of grievances that the Muslim world had against U.S. foreign policy. I volunteered, but I felt I had to. After opposing the 1991 Gulf War and the crippling U.S.-led economic sanctions against the Iraqi people—which led to perhaps hundreds of thousands of further deaths and an evisceration of civil society—and working for a just peace in Israel/Palestine, I knew very well why people in the Middle East would resent U.S. empire.

During the public event at my university, in the heady days after 9/11, I stood up and spoke—not to harangue my fellow citizens, but to deconstruct that "they hate us for our freedom," an idea that George W. Bush argued when he addressed the nation on September 20, 2001. It was not easy to stand up and point out all the ways that the United States was hardly innocent, given that so many were dead and the country was still reeling. My every utterance felt immediately political and connected intimately to how fellow Arabs and Arab Americans might be treated. Perhaps I could, I thought, say what they could not say. Though I will not joke about bombs over the phone, I know that I have certain rights as a citizen to speak my mind. Many first-generation Arab Americans and noncitizens do not share that confidence and live in terror of losing the hold they have on life here. What I did not say then, and can only admit to myself fifteen years later, is that I had the fleeting thought—alongside my confusion and grief—that the United States now could feel what others had felt because of our reckless imperialism abroad.

For many Arab American writers, 9/11 became a moment in which we "outed" ourselves—that is, claimed solidarity with fellow Arab Americans and with movements against oppression and injustice throughout the Arab world. But it's easy to overstate the importance of 9/11 to Arab American literature; since at least the 1980s, Arab American poets have negotiated a complex double-consciousness that translates and troubles both the American and Arab. Arab American poets such as Lawrence Joseph, Naomi Shihab Nye, Suheir Hammad, Mohja Kahf, Fady Joudah, Khaled Mattawa, Deema Shehabi, Hayan Charara, Marwa Helal, Safia Elhillo, and George Abraham attempt to re-write the Orientalist narrative of Arab life, engage in modes of political and aesthetic resistance, and worry their connection to and complicity with the nation. For these poets, a cosmopolitan vision of global citizenship is haunted by the knowledge of U.S. privilege and the national liberation struggles in the postcolonial Middle East.

Though Arab Americans—legally considered "white" but who often faced discrimination based on immigrant status and religious/cultural difference—often chose the path of quiet assimilation, Arab American writers did not long remain politically quiescent. Emboldened by the ethnic liberation movements and by the courageous work of Edward Said—whose landmark *Orientalism* (1978) was followed by groundbreaking critiques of empire, Zionism, and representations of Islam—Arab American poets such as D. H. Melhem, Lawrence Joseph, Naomi Shihab Nye, Samuel Hazo, Elmaz Abinader, and others began to write Arab American life in a way that began to get serious attention in the 1990s.

Steven Salaita noted the post-9/11 profusion of Arab American literature has come with a remarkably robust range. In his words, "there is no such thing as diversity in Arab America; there are diversities. We do not adhere to a singular body politic: we engage in all sorts of politics. We do not occupy an Arab American culture: we belong to numerous cultures."[1] Yet certain themes recur, as he notes: not only immigration and assimilation but also U.S. racism, xenophobia, and marginalization. And more particularly, Arab American literature returns to the paroxysm of the Israeli-Palestinian conflict, the Lebanese Civil War, Islam, and patriarchy/homophobia—all themes exacerbated and irritated by empire.

Read alongside *Orientalism*, Deleuze and Guattari's articulation of "minor literature" is a useful lens through which to examine Arab American poetry. For Deleuze and Guattari, the minority writer changes the language in which he works—the way, say, early African American musicians bent notes on the guitar to approximate African musical scales. In minor literature as well, the "cramped space [of the writer's world] forces each individual intrigue to connect immediately to politics. The individual concern thus becomes all the more necessary, indispensable, magnified, because a whole other story is vibrating within it."[2] This hyper-politicization is further pressurized by the ways in which the minority writer constantly writes not merely for herself but for a collective whose agency is compromised by its minority status. Finally, in minor literature, a writer's work is by its very being more than a privatized utterance; an "individuated enunciation" cannot "be separated from a collective enunciation."[3]

Arab American poetry compels a slight reordering, which emphasizes the problematics of reception and the politics of representation that complicate and often threaten Arab American subjectivity. First and foremost, there is the politicization of all things Arab. This politicization is inextricably connected to U.S. foreign policy in the Middle East, driven by the geopolitical thirst for oil and desire to support Israel and the Gulf States at almost any cost. Nearly every articulation or representation of the Israeli-Palestinian conflict must face the condemnatory force of Israel apologists and the smear of anti-Semitism, silencing dialogue. Arab American experience and the experience of other ethnic Americans are analogous, but the particularity of U.S. foreign policy toward the Middle East—which far predates the 9/11 attacks—is the backdrop against which Arab American literature finds itself.

Second, Orientalism, or the repertory of ready-made stereotypes about those in the Middle East, continues to haunt the U.S. imagination of Arabs. U.S. cultural, racial, and religious xenophobia rhyme with this Orientalism. This system of stereotyping, of course, provides the justification for an aggressive U.S. foreign policy that favors two primary material and geopolitical interests: oil and Israel. Recently, when I posted on Facebook a link to a performance by a young British Palestinian poet Rafeef Ziadah, a colleague who teaches at a local private high school noted that his "students are doing an oral poetry recitation as part of their final next week. How I'd love to share this and how I know I'd get run out of the building if I did. Too bad, for sure."

Given the politicization of all things Arab, Arab American writers cannot escape the pressure of the political and the desire to represent, as these anecdotes illustrate. They merely confirm what Jack Shaheen demonstrated in his landmark study, *Reel Bad Arabs* (2001), which analyzed 1,000 American films and found less than a dozen had positive, nuanced representations of Arabs.[4] In light of limited and limiting representations, Deleuze and Guattari's notion of minor literature privileges literature without "subject"—that which is "non-representative, deterritorializing."[5] Yet Arab American literature extends from mainstream modes all the way to that experimental horizon.

With the predominance of stereotypical representations in the mass media and popular culture, Arab American writers have had a lot of work to do, and therefore their use of mainstream poetic tactics of autobiographical lyric and anecdotal narrative seem as useful as experimental methods of minor literature. Some poets actively court the dangers of self-commodification and strategically employ dominant or mainstream poetic modes, such as Naomi Shihab Nye and Mohja Kahf. Others identify

43

with and employ African American strategies of engaged political poetry, such as Suheir Hammad. Others hybridize American poetry with Arab language and poetic traditions, such as
Hammad, Fady Joudah, Deema Shehabi, Hayan Charara, and
Marwa Helal. Still others attempt experimental assemblages of
collage, such as the recent work of Khaled Mattawa. In short,
Arab American poets have used *any means necessary*. But let's begin with Lawrence Joseph, whose poetry has evolved as his vision
of poetry's possibilities has dilated—from personal narrative to
prophetic critique of empire and global capital.

A lawyer from Detroit, Lawrence Joseph emerged in the
1980s as an important poet whose work was inflected by the
working class storytelling of Philip Levine and his own ethnic
roots. Joseph's fifth book of poems, *Into It* (2005), propelled
him into the position of visionary poet. These poems employ a
gyring consciousness that sees the war embedded in a geography of global capitalism, military specularity, and Old Testament
imagery. Here, Joseph explicitly implicates himself, as if he were
prophet and drone pilot:

Zoom in close enough—the shadows
of statues, the swimming pools of palaces . . .
closer—a garden of palm trees,
oranges and lemons, chickens, sheep . . .

Yes, that's it. I've become
too clear-sighted—the mechanics of power
are too transparent.[6]

Joseph's ability to situate himself in the place of complicity
marks his poetic project as particularly *American*, intriguingly assuming the position of citizen of empire at a time when Arab-
ness was suspect.

From the same generation, by contrast, Naomi Shihab Nye,
has worked to demonstrate the humanity of Arabs, both in the
lyrical representation of her nonviolent vision and in her narrative depictions of Arab and Arab American life. Shortly after
the 2001 terrorist attacks, Nye published an open letter "To Any
Would-Be Terrorists," demonstrating the particular pain that

these attacks caused Arab Americans, who had worked for years to be part of the fabric of a suspicious society.[7] Relatedly, she published a selection of her Arab-themed poems called *19 Varieties of Gazelle: Poems of the Middle East* (2002).[8] Even the title of the book is a testament of the beauty and diversity of Arab culture and being. To her credit, her work does not spare critique of American imperial meddling, outright censorship, and cultural ignorance, as a poem like "All Things *Not* Considered" aptly announces: "you cannot stitch the breath / back into this boy."[9] But the way she grounds her poetic depiction of Palestine so often through her beloved father, Aziz Shihab, in her elegiac *Transfer* (2011), makes it nearly impossible not to think of Aziz when one hears any story of Palestinian refugees. In "Scared, Scarred, Sacred," Nye writes of her father:

> All your life you were flying back to your lost life
> Dropping down like the Oz house.
> You kept the key, as Palestinians do.
> You kept the doorknocker.
> And now you are homeless for real.
> Fire ate your body, you became as big as the sky.[10]

It is commonplace among Palestinian refugees to have the keys to the houses from which they were exiled, along with title deeds and other papers, which bring them no closer to their desired return. Nye's familiarly American image—that of Dorothy's whirling house in *The Wizard of Oz*—enables Americans a way of feeling about Palestinian exile that evokes its utter strangeness. The final image—describing a cremation—at once feels like a liberatory release and an uneasy evocation of the Holocaust.

From a younger generation, Palestinian American poet Suheir Hammad began her poetry by employing a poetic style inspired by June Jordan and hip-hop, registering her identification between Arab American and African American oppression and political-cultural struggle: "carry continents in our eyes / survivors of the middle passage."[11] In *Born Palestinian, Born Black* (1996), Hammad's "Dedication" is a poetry of militant outrage, that

sees Palestine over the sea
feels her uncle's heart join hers
thinks of exchanging her books and pencil
for a knife a small pistol[12]

Her early poetic—like some Black Arts poetry—occasionally
slips into the posture of binary thinking: white/black, evil/
good, Israeli/Palestinian, etc. If, in the words of Deleuze and
Guattari, "the political domain has contaminated every statement,"[13] Hammad's early work suffers, at times, from the pressure of the political. However, by the time she began to appear
on HBO's Def Poetry Jam just after 9/11, her work gained intimacy and authority, traversing its distance between audiences more nimbly; through her compelling performances, Arab
American poetry and culture reached new audiences. Her role
in popular culture marked a sea change from the narratives of
self-orientalism and proposes that Arab American identity is by
no means uncomplex. In fact, *breaking poems* (2008) moves close
to minor literature in its syncretic combinations of Arabic and
English, in its globalist broken embodiments: "moon / same in
ramallah wa new orleans wa jerusalem wa johannesburg wa beirut same moon."[14] The "wa" simply means "and" in Arabic, but
its repetitions begin to sound like a suturing cry.

Published in the same year as the hoax-text *Honor Lost,* Mohja
Kahf's *Emails from Scheherazad* (2003) supplements Hammad's
radical ferocity with poignantly comical portrayals of Arab American feminist subjectivity. In "My Grandmother Washes Her Feet
in the Sink of the Bathroom at Sears," as I discussed in a previous essay, Kahf re-creates the comic-awkward panic of trying to
explain her grandmother's ablutions to scandalized Midwestern
women. The global reach of the grandmother's practice extends
back, in Kahf's poem, to Aleppo, Damascus, and Istanbul, and
relies upon the porcelain of China—widening our cultural sense
of what cleanliness might mean and how cultural practices are
rarely narrowly nationalistic.[15]

Fady Joudah's *The Earth in the Attic* (2008), the first Arab
American winner of the Yale Younger Poets prize, centrally concerns itself with life in exile. The son of Palestinian refugees,

Joudah's style blends hard-edged poetic witness with the dream-like evanescence of Mahmoud Darwish. Joudah composes a narrative poetry that defies the linearity of dull narration; instead, he braids multiple lines of narrative, enacting multiple departures and longed-for returns of the exiled.

In "Along Came a Spider," Joudah references those early morning moments where the earth is secured for the spider to create its web, its home-space:

> On mornings of this refugee settlement,
> After the rain falls in stalks
> Of mushroom clouds,
> The spiders bloom anywhere there's a web-hold
> And the earth is like an attic.[16]

Like Walt Whitman in "A Noiseless Patient Spider," Joudah sees the spider as a slightly ludicrous figure of the indomitable faith of home-seeking in an inhospitable world. In this poem, the "refugee settlement" resonates doubly, as both an African and a Palestinian experience seen simultaneously.

This double-resonance happens hauntingly in "Scarecrow," as if the poet's work for Doctors Without Borders in Zambia and the Sudan somehow were a repetition of family history. The refugees have "no time to look for anyone," and are nearly run over by army trucks, yet:

> Later, they will accuse you of giving up your land.
>
> Later, you will stand in distribution lines and won't receive
>   enough to eat.
> Your mother will weave you new underwear from flour sacks.
>
> And they'll give you plastic tents, cooking pots,
> Vaccine cards, white pills, and wool blankets.
>
> And you will keep your cool.
> Standing with eyes shut tight like you've got soap in them,
>
> Arms stretched wide like you're catching rain.[17]

Though the opening of the book focuses principally from the point of view of a doctor treating refugees in Africa (in the harrowing sequence "Pulse"), the poems of the second section deliver the hauntingly palimpsestic trauma, where these two conflicts (Darfur and Palestine) come to resemble each other—though one is widely termed a genocide and the other something else. Joudah's ethical delicacy is to avoid "The Name of the Place" (as one poem is called)—but also to refuse to exoticize or reify what Darfur has come to represent in American liberal consciousness. In this refusal of names, he refuses the gradations of suffering—that some events are tragedies, others atrocities, that some policies are civil wars, others genocides.

We can see the sudden solidarities between exiled people—whether displaced Arab Americans or Africans—in Joudah's very first poem, where a taxi driver notes that if one sees the hoopoe as a good omen, "you are one of us."[18] Identity is fluid, and what we believe and who we stand with can be as important as who we are or how others think of us. Khaled Mattawa, in his essay "Freeways and Rest Houses" from the anthology *Post Gibran*, has called for an Arab American literature that moves beyond post-assimilation nostalgia and post-Gibran self-orientalism. In his words,

> the staples of grandmotherly aphorism, thickly accented patriarchal traditionalism, culinary nostalgia, religious dogma, belly dancing and adoration of Kahlil Gibran are meager nourishments for cultural identity, let alone a cultural revival and a subsequent engagement with the larger American culture.[19]

Avoiding the safe ethnic-identity tropes of food and family, Mattawa has begun to create in his own poetry the answer to his critical call.

Tocqueville (2010), Mattawa's fourth book of poems, enters the philosophical territory of Lawrence Joseph's *Into It*, meditating on what it means to be a poet at the center of American power. But *Tocqueville*, in contrast to Mattawa's lyrically driven previous work, pronounces that it no longer suffices to sing, even to sing of dark times. Rather, through the experimentally daring poetry

of Mattawa—born in Libya and for years an American citizen—
we become witnesses to our own implicatedness, our own vul-
nerable privilege.[20]

While the first poem is entitled "Lyric"—and begins, "Will answers be found / like seeds / planted among rows of song?"[21]—
the lyric "I" of the poet pulses through the entire collection,
through its wider networks of imperial history, global economic
flows, and Machiavellian politics, emerging in the diverse voices
of a Somali singer, a Sierra Leonean victim/perpetrator of atrocity, a gallery viewer of photographs of Palestinian exile, a factory
worker in Georgia, Ecclesiastes as insurance salesman, a terrorist, a State Department insider.

The keynote poem of the book is "On the Difficulty of Docu-
mentation," a dialogic meditation on the role of art in a world
of violence. The poem takes as its mediating occasion a photo-
graphic exhibit of Palestinian refugees. Here, Mattawa quotes
liberally from two poets, as if in dialogue: Sir Thomas Wyatt, of
the Renaissance courtly love tradition, and Bertolt Brecht, of the
school of alienation and political action. As the poem reflects
on the refugee pictures, Mattawa zigs and zags between poetry's
desire to herald the beautiful and its desire to be truthful—
between art and history, between transcendence and wound.
It ends with Wyatt rather than Brecht, but such a tilt does not
suggest that beauty wins. The deft collage of photographs and
poetry quotes builds, until Wyatt's own words—"they flee from
me"—becomes more than a courtly love elegy:

And what of that look, and the all too human?

To be enthralled

   and fain know what she hath deserved (Wyatt)

   the squalor that makes the brow grow stern
     the just anger that turns a voice harsh. (Brecht)

What else could she do, as she parts, but softly say,

   Oh dear heart, how like you this? (Wyatt)[22]

In the end, Wyatt's lament becomes a lament of the political poet, who sees the refugees themselves disappear from his language, from the wider narrative of human rights, displaced by a state that was meant to instantiate the rights of another genocided people.

Tocqueville's central poem, "Tocqueville"—which includes many of the voices referenced above—is a tour-de-force globalist polyphonic collage, extending over twenty-six pages. Here, we feel the poet linger on the dark abyss of globalization—how its purported connectedness has come with profound alienation. Mattawa recreates the poet's role as global Tocqueville, but this prophetic Tocqueville has none of the adoring tone of the original Frenchman; he has seen too much. Instead, among other things, we witness to the words of a man who is compelled by soldiers to beat his baby son to death:

> They found me in the house with my baby child. They'd already killed my wife in the field. They told me to place the child in the mortar we used to mash cassava. Then they handed me the club and told me to bludgeon my child, or they would kill me. And I did as they said. Afterwards, they cut off both my arms and let me go.[23]

In this poem, Brechtian alienation trumps the poet's longing for the beautiful. *Tocqueville* is a lyric that repudiates lyricism, an unrepeatable experiment, a witness to blindness, a shooting script without camera or bullet. Mattawa takes no cynical distance from the operations of empire; he situates himself, and all of us, in the middle of it, and asks us not to look away but to lean in and bear its weighty implications.

It would be impossible to avoid the Israeli-Palestinian issue in a discussion of Arab American poetry. One of the more poignant aspects of the Israeli-Palestinian conflict is how the existence of the Jewish state attenuates the rich history of Jewish cosmopolitan thinking as it has produced yet another experience of exile—for Palestinians. *Diaspo/Renga* (2014), a collaborative sequence written by Marilyn Hacker and Deema Shehabi, offers a paradigmatic cosmopoetic example of how Jewish and

Palestinian experience of exile provides a window into imaginative empathy for and identification with oppressed and displaced peoples throughout the world. Hacker—the celebrated poet and expatriate American Jew who's the leading translator of Arab Francophone poetry—began an email correspondence with Palestinian American poet Deema Shehabi, in the Japanese form called "renga." From the very first alternating exchanges, the poets lift and shift our gaze from site to site, and from sight to sight, beginning in Gaza, the archetypal geography of immobility and imprisonment:

Five, six—and righteous,
the child in green in Gaza
stands in her wrecked home,

grubby, indignant. Her hands
point; she explains what was done

bombed, burned. It all smells
like gas! We had to throw our clothes
away! The earrings my

father gave me . . . No martyr,
resistant. The burnt cradle . . .

breaks over the cold mountains
of North Carolina where a Cherokee
poet huddles in a cottage

by an indigo fire. She sees
the child and says:

This is the new Trail of Tears.
Calls out: Oh outspread Indian nation
let's braid our hair

with the pulverized
gravel of Palestine.

Witness, she says, the unpinned
knuckles of this child. Feel
the burlap curtains whip across . . .

the third floor window
in Belleville, dyed blue-purple
like the hyacinth

on the windowsill. Nedjma
does math homework. Strike today;

but school tomorrow.
Coming back from the demo
they sang in the street—

Rêve Générale!—the slogan
makes her smile. Wan winter sun . . .[24]

Hacker initiates our journey in Gaza, where a child becomes
spokesperson for the depredations of Israeli bombing, and
Shehabi—whose grandfather was once the mayor of Gaza—
sends us to North Carolina, where a Cherokee poet sees this
child (presumably on television or in a news story) and sutures
her own experience of dispossession (the "Trail of Tears" to the
Palestinian *Nakba*). The connection between colonialisms has
been a regular motif in Palestinian literature, famously in Mahmoud Darwish's "Address of the Red Indian." Then, almost as
quickly, Hacker brings us back to her Paris, richly populated by
Arabs such as Nedjma, and the city's vital tradition of general
strikes.

Hacker and Shehabi cocreate a meeting place in poetic language of their multiple word-worlds, inflected by exile but not
silenced by it. When Shehabi writes of the experience of reading Arabic to Hacker, a student of Arabic, they meet in the raw
sensuality of the lips and teeth and tongue and ear.

For Arab American poetry, cosmopolitan belonging is always
complicated by the very real vulnerabilities and griefs of the
refugee, of the exile who, in the words of Hacker and Shehabi,
"grabs a fistful of ground."[25] Though any place can come to be
called home, Arab American poetry contains a thirst for connec-

tion to belonging and place that urban cosmopolitanism cannot slake.

The cosmopolitanism that Ameen Rihani aimed for in the first salvo of Arab American literature, *The Book of Khalid* (1911), remains the direction toward which some of the best of Arab American poetry is now tending.[26] But we must continue to distinguish such globality or cosmopoetics from mere cheerleading for globalization, neoliberalism and empire. On the contrary, critically engaged globalism does not reject the idea of the nation-state, nor does it accept the so-called Clash of Civilizations. Given the ongoing colonialism in Israel-Palestine, the failure of the Arab Spring in Egypt, the rise of ISIS, and the civil war in Syria, the poetic cosmopolitanism of Arab American poetry necessarily holds a space for the work of national liberation.

Since 2001, Arab American poets have written against the fear-mongering of empire, "inclined to speak" (the title of a crucial Arab American poetry anthology) against the Orientalism of our time.[27] In *Something Sinister* (2016), Hayan Charara sutures Middle East and Middle America, American English and Arab American realities. In his wrenching poem "Animals," the abused dog that the speaker rescues in America turns into a meditation on the cruel violence of the Israel-Lebanon War in 2006, in which his young brother mourns his murdered pets. After describing the eviscerated bodies of these beloved animals, the poem ends:

> Look. They're animals.
> Which is to say,
> there are also people.
> And I haven't even
> begun telling you
> what was done to them.[28]

Charara's poem surprises at every turn and, on the way, undoes many Orientalist and imperial clichés: that all Muslims find dogs dirty, that our technowars have little collateral damage, that the people of the Middle East are cruel animals. After all, these dead were made by America's allies. In its final lines, the poem marks powerfully those who are disappeared by the imperial narrative of the war.

Recent works of a new generation of Arab American poets such as Marwa Helal, Safia Elhillo, and George Abraham embrace bilinguality and bring Arabic language and poetry into American poetry in surprising ways. Helal's invention of "the Arabic" poetic form (a poem that's read from right to left), Elhillo's employment of Arabic, and Abraham's explosive experiments with the page stretch Arab American poetry in new directions, while retaining the tradition's fierce commitment to resisting imperial violence and erasure.

"All our wars," as Maxine Hong Kingston wrote after 9/11, "are civil wars," since the United States contains peoples from every nation in the world.[29] The ongoing wars in the Middle East compel us to remind Americans that humanity does not end at the national border and to interrogate all "comfort zones" in light of "conflict zones." Arab American poets will continue to play a key role in confronting the imperial temperament, reminding us that the machinations of power are neither distant nor without consequence. Poetry may not stop tanks or drone attacks, but Arab American poetry can leap the gulf between the dominant narrative of the United States and the realities experienced on the ground. Denial is not a river in Egypt, and it's not just residual anger from the shadows of the Twin Towers. It's also the ideological blindness of imperial privilege, supplemented by Orientalism. What Arab American poets show us is a way to see again through our unclarity of vision—through empathic identification, provocative confrontation, the tonic of comedy, the honesty of confession, the collage of subaltern voices, the melding of Arabic and American language and poetry. What we do with this new sight is another question entirely.

Notes

1. Steven Salaita, *Arab American Literary Fictions, Cultures, Politics* (New York: Palgrave Macmillan, 2007), 2.
2. Gilles Deleuze and Felix Guattari, "What Is a Minor Literature?" in *Kafka: Toward a Minor Literature* (Minneapolis: University of Minnesota Press, 1986), 17.
3. Ibid.

4. Jack Shaheen, *Reel Bad Arabs: How Hollywood Vilifies a People* (Northampton: Olive Branch Press, 2001).

5. Deleuze and Guattari, *Kafka: Toward a Minor Literature*, 21.

6. Lawrence Joseph, "Rubaiyat," in *Into It* (New York: Farrar, Straus & Giroux, 2005b), 41.

7. Naomi Shihab Nye, "To Any Would-Be Terrorists," in *September 11, 2001: American Writers Respond*, ed. William Heyen (Silver Springs: Etruscan, 2002), 287–91.

8. Naomi Shihab Nye, *19 Varieties of Gazelle: Poems of the Middle East* (New York: Greenwillow Books, 2002).

9. Ibid., 133.

10. Naomi Shihab Nye, "Scared, Scarred, Sacred," in *Transfer* (Rochester: Boa Editions, 2011), 23.

11. Suheir Hammad, "open poem to those who rather we not read . . . or breathe," in *Born Palestinian, Born Black* (New York: Harlem Rivers Press, 1996), 81.

12. Suheir Hammad, "Dedication," in *Born Palestinian, Born Black* (New York: Harlem Rivers Press, 1996), 13.

13. Deleuze and Guattari, *Kafka: Toward a Minor Literature*, 17.

14. Suheir Hammad, *breaking poems* (New York: Cypher Books, 2008), 34.

15. Kahf, Mohja, "My Grandmother Washes Her Feet in the Sink of the Bathroom at Sears," in *Emails from Scheherazad* (Gainesville: University Press of Florida, 2003).

16. Fady Joudah, "Along Came a Spider," in *The Earth in the Attic* (New Haven: Yale University Press, 2008), 57.

17. Ibid., 45.

18. Joudah, "Atlas," 3.

19. Khaled Mattawa, "Freeways and Rest Houses," in *Post Gibran: Anthology of New Arab American Writing*, ed. Munir Akash and Khaled Mattawa (Syracuse: Syracuse University Press/Kitab, 2000), 61.

20. Khaled Mattawa, *Tocqueville* (Kalamazoo: New Issues Press, 2010).

21. Ibid., 2.

22. Ibid., 5.

23. Ibid., 29.

24. Marilyn Hacker and Deema Shehabi, *Diaspo/Renga: A Collaboration in Alternating Renga* (London: Holland Park Press, 2014), 8–10.

25. Ibid.

26. Ameen Rihani, *The Book of Khalid* (New York: Melville House, 1911).

27. Hayan Charara, ed., *Inclined to Speak: Contemporary Arab American Poetry* (Fayetteville: University of Arkansas Press, 2009).

28. Hayan Charara, *Something Sinister* (Pittsburgh, PA: Carnegie Mellon, 2016).

29. Maxine Hong Kingston, quoted in Richard Grey, "Imagining the Crisis in Drama and Poetry," in *After the Fall: American Literature Since 9/11* (Hoboken: Wiley-Blackwell, 2011), 184.

Khalil Gibran
Local Boy Made Good

The first thing that you learn about Khalil Gibran from an Arab, particularly a Lebanese immigrant in love with the Old Country, is that his name is not Khalil Gibran. Nor is it, as my edition of *The Prophet* has it, "Kahlil Gibran."[1] He was born Gibrān Khalīl Gibrān bin Mikhā'īl bin Sa'ad. It's typical for an immigrant to the New World to shed some of the flourishes of an Old World name, so its Ellis-Island-style reduction is not so surprising. However, the spelling of his first name still mystifies me; in Arabic, the sound that we transliterate as "kh" is an aspirated "h" so the displacement of the "h"—which appears not only on his books but also on his letterhead—is but one of many "lost in translation" moments of the boy from Bsharri.

A few years ago, in a review of Gibran biographies in *The New Yorker*, Joan Acocella notes that Gibran's publishing numbers for his ubiquitous *The Prophet* (1923) place him third all-time among poets, after Shakespeare and Lao-tzu, selling over nine million copies in the United States. Yet his pop culture prowess—first blooming in the 1930s and then again with the 1960s counterculture—moves beyond the books:

> There are public schools named for Gibran in Brooklyn and Yonkers. "The Prophet" has been recited at countless weddings and funerals. It is quoted in books and articles on training art teachers, determining criminal responsibility, and enduring ectopic pregnancy, sleep disorders, and the news that your son is gay. Its words turn up in advertisements for marriage counsellors, chiropractors, learning-disabilities specialists, and face cream.[2]

If Acocella's tone is lightly mocking, contemporary poets are relentless in their derision of Gibran, placing his poetry somewhere between Jewel and Jimmy Carter.

But Gibran was a revered name in my household, and in my father's childhood home in Brooklyn, not only because he was a Lebanese poet who wrote the ubiquitous *The Prophet* but also because he hailed from the hometown of my father's grandmother: Bsharri, Lebanon. He came to stay at their home in Brooklyn Heights (290 Hicks Street) in the 1920s, and according to family legend, wrote some of his *Prophet* while there.

I can't confirm that story, though it's been repeated in guidebooks of Brooklyn. (My uncle sent me a PDF of the page on Brooklyn Heights that mentions that fact, but when we contacted the author, she told him the source: it was someone else from our family.) Still, I love this legend. It's redolent of the myth-building that I love about my father's side, who, like all immigrant families, suffered the great reduction of assimilation mostly in silence, pressing their bodies against the warm shared wall of the neighbors because they didn't have enough money for coal in the winter.

What I do have is a copy of the letter of thanks that Gibran wrote to my great-grandmother for her generosity in having him stay with them. Whatever else you want to say about Gibran, he was a local boy made good. And, in the process of blazing his trail from Bsharri, gave Arab Americans and Arab American poets a figure of their own possible success in translating ineffable Bsharris into poetic Brooklyns.

Gibran's "masterpiece," such as it is, turns not so much upon poetry as upon the genre of wisdom literature, and its subgenre, the aphorism, which holds a particularly valued place in Arab culture, and is indebted strongly to the first Arab American novel, *The Book of Khalid* (1911), by Ameen Rihani.

"You really ought to read this book," my great-uncle Fred wrote to me in his letter accompanying a PDF-version of *The Book of Khalid*, in the years before a centenary edition was released by Melville House. Fred was born Farid, the youngest of nine children in the Boulos household, and the one who remembered pressing his body against the warm shared wall of the neighbors. Based on Rihani's experience of immigration from

Lebanon, the story follows Khalid, a muleboy who transforms first into a peddler (of fake Holy Land trinkets), then into a political activist, and finally into revolutionary mystic and martyr. Khalid is an Arab Quixote, day-dreaming of love and honor and therefore constantly suffering indignities from the cruel and the powerful. By the end, he turns from being a lovelorn muleboy into a true visionary, returning to Syria. It's a brilliant, wise, and comical take on the complexities of immigration and on the desire to marry East and West.

Gibran was friends with Ameen Rihani, part of *Arrabitah*, or the Pen League, the first flourishing of Arab American letters during the birth of modernism. Gibran provided original illustrations for *The Book of Khalid*, and it's impossible not to hear an Ur version of Gibran's prophet in Khalid, who would come to coin such aphorisms as "if your hopes are not crucified, you pass into the Paradise of your dreams. If they are crucified . . . the gates of the said Paradise will be shut against you."[3]

A decade after *The Book of Khalid*, Gibran published *The Prophet*; the frame of the story is flimsier than Rihani's, less wrought with literary self-irony; in it, the sage Almustafa, who has been living in exile in Orphalese, is called upon by the people to share his wisdom on various questions of life: love, marriage, children, giving, eating and drinking, work, etc. The meat of the book is comprised of the aphoristic prose poems on these themes. Like all good aphorists, Gibran uses language in a way that is both plain and metaphorical; it invites understanding, yet in a way that brushes against the ineffable. On the pain that is part of love, Gibran strikes sharply:

> When love beckons to you, follow him,
> Though his ways are hard and steep.
> And when his wings enfold you yield to him,
> Though the sword hidden among his pinions may wound
> you.
> And when he speaks to you believe in him,
> Though his voice may shatter your dreams as the north wind
> lays waste the garden . . .
>
> But if in your fear you would seek only love's peace and
> love's pleasure,

> Then it is better for you that you cover your nakedness and
> pass out of love's threshing-floor,
> Into the seasonless world where you shall laugh, but not all
> of your laughter, and weep, but not all of your tears . . .[4]

Say what you will about the familiarity of the images or the occasionally wooden phrasings, dear reader: what I know of love is in this. How the most intimate relationships can be the cause of our greatest joy and greatest suffering, and yet in the holding-back from such intimacies, some essential salt of life seems absent. If poetry is a tuning-toward the mystery of what it means to be alive, then this is poetry.

There's no doubt that Gibran's style occasionally ascends into unintentionally comic elevations—with its anachronistic Victorianisms—and its high and earnest tone seems out of place in the ironies and specificities of American life. And arguably its success is partly related to the self-Orientalizing of its author, whose earnest "Eastern" persona seems right out of a footnote from Edward Said.

But the spiritual homelessness, the raw longing that resonates past the cliché, describes and embodies what I've felt of immigrant life. I think of the liquid melancholy in my grandmother's eyes shining back at me when I would visit her at 290 Hicks Street, filled with some kind of impossible-to-quench thirst, a look I've seen so often when meeting immigrants and refugees and exiles from all directions of the compass. In the eyes of the Nguyen family in San Diego that came to be part of our family, fleeing the Vietnam War. In the eyes of the Russians I know, rousting about in Chicago and Cleveland. In the eyes of my Palestinian friends, flung the four directions, generation after generation.

On houses, for example, the Prophet says:

> Your house shall be not an anchor but a mast.
> It shall not be a glistening film that covers a wound, but an
> eyelid that guards the eye.[5]

I love that metaphor; that the house is not a staying-put but a vehicle for movement by standing still. A place to close the eyes, to dream, and to open them again. An immigrant is just a person who knows home is a verb.

Speaking of houses, here's the letter Gibran sent to my great-grandmother, Nehia Boulos, thanking her for hosting him at 290 Hicks Street, in rough translation:

Kahlil Gibran
51 West 10th St.
New York, City
April 22, 1927

To the Woman of My Country,

I salute you with a thousand salutes. I was very happy receiving your second letter, this is due to missing your first letter between my going to Boston and getting back to New York and could not find your address among my papers, and there are so many of them in this room.

I beg your pardon and forgiveness. You will know that every breeze from our Old Country breezes takes me back to that high mountain and that holy valley, you and your family and all that surround you are from these delightful breezes.

In every season I leave to Boston, leaving all my works behind me. This is because I prefer to be around people who were from where I was born and . . . they are like me and sincere to this beautiful far country.

I beg you first to best wishes to your kind husband and children (old and young) (God bless them), and second to mention my name with kindness to your dear parents, and to your relatives. They are, like you well are, related to me. The same blood that flows in their veins flows through mine too.

God bless you and protect you, from the sincere son of your country,

Khalil Gibran

The letter has the kind of poetic language that is typical not only of a poet but also of the Arabic language as well. But the poetry of the letter is not explained by Arabic language only. In the dedication to my copy of *The Prophet*, given on my 20th birthday, my father writes, in English: "you are a prophet yourself and a distant cousin of Kahlil. If you could take in complete the pride and love other people have of you, you would be an even happier young man." Acocella, later in her review, notes "a later mentor declared him a mystic, "a young prophet" before he'd published a word. "And so he began to see himself that way."[6]

I, too, was baptized into the possibility of self-mythology. It was a gift, I see now, to have the sort of parents willing to see prophecy in a vexatious, self-conscious, over-serious and dreamy child. I would read the book gingerly, as if afraid of its influence. Later, I would come to write poems that my father would claim were the first he ever really understood as poems, because they told the stories of his family. (My mother, by contrast, always loved poetry and liked to quote Wordsworth, Hopkins, and Eliot.) Still later, I would write a book about the Iraq War that would leave both of my parents in varying states of panic and confusion, wondering if the book's obsession with torture was secretly really *about me.*

Yet to this day, my father marvels over my lines, wondering aloud who precisely could have written them, and if I did, whether I was indeed his child. As Gibran would have it, via the Prophet's words: "Your children are not your children . . . You are the bows from which your children as living arrows are sent forth."[7]

Notes

1. Kahlil Gibran, *The Prophet* (New York: Alfred A. Knopf, 1989).

2. Joan Acocella, "Prophet Motive: The Kahlil Gibran Phenomenon," *The New Yorker,* January 7, 2008.

3. Ameen Rihani, *The Book of Khalid* (New York: Dodd, Mead and Co., 1911).

4. Gibran, *The Prophet,* 12.

5. Ibid., 33.

6. Joan Acocella, "Prophet Motive."

7. Gibran, *The Prophet,* 18.

(More) News from Poems
Investigative/Documentary/Social Poetics[1]
(2017)

"It is difficult / to get the news from poems / Yet men die miserably every day / for lack / of what is found there."[2] These familiar lines from William Carlos Williams' "Asphodel, That Greeny Flower," so often summoned in the defense of poetry's value, argue against viewing poetry as reported news. Yet Williams, most notably in *Paterson*, and many other modern and contemporary poets—from the "Objectivists" to hip-hop artists—have sought to marry poetry with the news, to translate that "news" into a wider history of human struggle for liberation. Drawing from the ballad tradition, modernist experiments with collage, documentary photography and film, jazz riffing, and hip-hop sampling, contemporary poets have increasingly begun to employ documentary materials to amplify the voices of people and movements that mass media journalism has tended to ignore or misrepresent. In this sense, they embody earlier lines in "Asphodel": "my heart rouses / thinking to bring you news / of something // that concerns you / and concerns many men."[3]

In 2007, "From Reznikoff to Public Enemy" appeared on the Poetry Foundation website. Since then, documentary poetry has become an increasingly widespread mode of poetic production, not only in the United States but around the world, with translations of the original essay appearing in Russian, Spanish, and Arabic. Given the interest of poets and readers of poetry in documentary poetry and the outpouring of documentary poetry, I've revisited the original essay here by expanding it to include works that have appeared in the past ten years. As both a critic and practitioner of such poetry, I hope that this intervention might clarify and complicate the stakes in documentary and investigative poetics.

That begins, of course, with the question of naming. The practitioners themselves vary in what they call this engagement with other texts and textualities: documentary poetry, investigative poetics, poetics of inquiry, research-based poetics, or social poetics—all overlapping practices, each with its own figuration of the poet: poet as alternative historian, detective, philosopher, radical text-worker, etc. These practices—which revolve around the conscious (and socially conscious) appropriation and adaptation of other texts—are not merely modernist, though the dominant methods tend to privilege these techniques. Though documentary poems sometimes echo and mimic legal discourse, historical accounts, or victim testimonies, what makes them vital is how they call upon the ancient and primal role of the poet in the community. Whether a poem such as a cento or a poem of "witness" would count as a documentary poem matters less than how it situates itself within its imagined community, the conversation of poetry itself. For me, the best documentary poems draw us back to the headwaters of poetry, where tribal elders, griots, troubadours, holy fools, tricksters, medicine men, witches, and shamans all do their work, comforting the afflicted and afflicting the comfortable.

Yes, my list of precursors simmers with contradiction. An elder may have one sort of story to tell, a trickster quite another. The work of an historian might open us to what Emerson called "the mind of the past" in a way entirely different from a shaman's practice and access point to the spirit world. Yet, this is the range represented by the broad band of documentary poetics and its aims—from historical recovery projects to rituals of healing trauma, from reasoned political interventions to subversive deconstructions.

I'd like to make three propositions, then, about documentary poetry and investigative poetics. First, to use Rukeyser's words, the poem can "extend the document," thus giving second life to lost or expurgated histories, yet still finally remaining a poem. In this outcome, the documentary poem offers its readers a double-movement, both inside the life of the poem and outside the poem. Documentary poetics arises from the idea that poetry is not a museum-object to be observed from afar but a dynamic medium that informs and is informed by history. The investigative poem opposes the idea of a poem as a closed system, inviting "the real life outside the poem" into the poem, offering readers a double-journey—one that takes them further into the poem and beyond its limits. It is the place of meeting between materiality and the imagination. Because of this double-movement, documentary poems constantly court their own collapse, testing the tensile boundaries of a poem in the face of what Wallace Stevens called "the pressure of reality," by which he meant "life in a state of violence, not physically violent as yet for us in America [sic], but physically violent for millions of our friends and for still millions of our enemies and spiritually violent, it may be said, for everyone else." Stevens never sounded so much like Martin Luther King. The successful documentary poem withstands the pressure of reality to remain a poem in its own right: its language and form cannot be reduced to an ephemeral broadside ready-made for its moment and then for the recycling bin. While it may be that such poems will not "stand up" in a court of law, they testify to the often-unheard voices of people struggling to survive in the face of unspeakable violence.

Second, the poem itself can be extended through the document, given a breadth or authority that the lyric utterance cannot attain on its own. Documentary poetry comes out of a desire to break open what has often been seen as the monology of the lyric. While the lyric at its best can be subtly dialogic, negotiating self and other in nuanced ways, documentary poets are drawn to the chorale effect, employing multiple voices and voicings that merge into a larger (but often dissonant) symphony. Documentary and investigative poems that don't simply "contain multitudes," as Whitman boasted, but breathe and seethe multitudes. One reason for the dramatic rise of documentary and investigative poetics may be that this poetry calls us back to poetic modes that twentieth-century poetry had appeared to have abandoned—the epic and the dramatic. At its most fundamental—and here, I will gloss only briefly what is an enormously varied and complex tradition—the epic poem emerged from the oral tradition of poetic storytelling, in which the sweeping narrative of a nation or people would be told. The early epics were amalgamations of poetry, politics, and history, and at their best, they offered both heroism and reflection. They didn't merely transmit history or heroic values; they offered a mirror on the culture, inviting their listeners to pose questions that the poems themselves could not answer. By contrast, in American poetry, as in American society, too often the lyric became privatized—that is, not merely private, but sealed off from the social and political realms. The intimacy of the lyric voice, fused with the narrative scope of the epic mode, has offered poets a way to envision and articulate their bodily and textual experiences in dialogue with the communities and societies in which they find themselves, their nations.

Third, and finally, the practice of investigative poetics extends the very idea of poetry, enabling a rethinking of what poetry is and what it can do; in this sense, it returns to a more fundamental and primal relationship to its audience. Documentary and investigative poetries come out of the sense that we are called to be cocreators of history through language and action: at times we wrestle with it (Jacob); at times we are consumed by it and then thrust out of it (Jonah); and at still other times we try to outlast its madness (Job). I employ these Biblical allusions not to delimit the scope of documentary poetry but rather to evoke how the practice of documentary poetics—that is, what leads us to dive into the detritus of the past or into repressed or oppressed moments or people or creatures in dominant narratives—necessarily places the poet into primal relation with otherness (angels and creatures and the divine), the otherness of others, the marginalized, the silenced, alongside or within the agents of empire, colonization, and erasure. In the words of Donovan Kūhiō Colleps: "documentary poetics has ways of inverting the colonial/imperial power of documents."

In contrast to certain tendencies in the conceptual poetry movement, which parallels and often overlaps investigative poetics, most practitioners of documentary and investigative poetics advocate for an ethical treatment of texts that carry the traces of lost or othered voices. In *Tracking/Teaching: On Documentary Poetics* (Essay Press, 2015), Camille Dungy writes of explorations of nineteenth-century American history for *Suck on the Marrow* in the context of the plagiaries of popular historians Doris Kearns Goodwin and Stephen Ambrose; the question of ethical sourcing drove her practice.[4] Similarly, Craig Santos Perez notes that documentary poetics "feels like a way to humbly enter into this immensely deep tradition moʻelelo, today."[5] Adrian Matejka puts it this way: "it's a matter of negotiating their spaces [of prominent African Americans and their stories] with respect and awareness, of honoring their lives."[6] Kaia Sand talks of "inexpert investigation," alongside Allison Cobb's resistance to what Ed Sanders calls "the air of mastery."[7]

It's for good reason that these poets worry about exploitation of texts. At the heart of documentary poetics—as at the heart of modernism—is the question of appropriation. The modernist notion that "good artists borrow, but great artists steal" cannot but sound like rationalizing exploitation and colonizing, given the modernist backdrop of European empire. So many disciplined, disappeared, and dismembered bodies. The latest outrage in this line of exploitation is Kenneth Goldsmith's conceptual poem "The Body of Michael Brown,"[8] an edited version of the autopsy of Michael Brown, whose murder by police led to months of protest and has been part of a wider social movement to reform policing in black communities and to expose institutionalized racism in law enforcement. In the words of Rin Johnson, "what I mean is there are political realities from which art cannot hide. To take a document like this and attempt to make it into a form of art is blatantly not engaging with the issues at hand."[9] Others critics have linked Goldsmith's conceptual piece with white supremacy itself.

The documentary poet who attempts to represent or "give voice" to the other (with all well-meaning and liberal intentions) necessarily must confront the epistemological limits that Gayatri Spivak articulates in "Can the Subaltern Speak?" Western attempts to represent "the other" almost invariably contain an epistemic violence. The very claim of a universality reinstantiates the subaltern position of the subaltern.[10] To put it another way: there is an ethical bind at the core of any documentary poetry project that attempts to reclaim history as some totality, or that says this is the body. The writers of investigative poetry must constantly confront both their epistemological limitedness and their positions of privilege as text-workers, as makers in the language of contemporary empire.

Documentary and investigative poetics situates itself on the dialectic between historicity and the transhistorical, between the local and the synechdocal, between the propaedeutic and the deconstructive, between the raw facticity of texts and bodies and the violence of the frame. The strengths of documentary poetry (its attention to preserving a history, its instructionality, its architectures) also risk the violence of silencing, naming, and excluding that the documentary poetry attempts to redress. Yet to refuse to engage in a dialogue with the silenced, to refuse to engage with the past, is also problematic for its own reasons. There is no getting around the past. James Baldwin once wrote, "To accept one's past—one's history—is not the same thing as drowning in it; it is learning how to use it."[11] I myself have an occasional tendency to feel like I'm drowning in the trauma of history, when the point is to learn to tread water, swim back to shore. History itself is a repository not only of the atrocious but also of the just and the beautiful. As Howard Zinn proposed:

> If history is to be creative, to anticipate a possible future without denying the past, it should, I believe, emphasize new possibilities by disclosing those episodes of the past when, even if in brief flashes, people showed their ability to resist, to join together, occasionally to win. I am supposing, or perhaps only hoping, that our future may be found in the past's fugitive moments of compassion rather than in its solid centuries of warfare.[12]

In Allison Cobb's words, "investigation is not only a way of looking back, a retracing. . . . Investigation is a way of asking how, now, to be alive."[13]

So, where to begin? What is the point of origin for this tradition?

In the beginning is the beginning of the Frame. In Mark Nowak's words, "the basic form is the frame."[14] Wherever one begins, something is cut out. The first lesson of documentary and investigative poetics, for me, is to pay attention to what is being left out, shorn away, effaced, suppressed. One could begin with balladeers as a starting point for a list of documentary poetry, particularly if one opens a space for rich topical verse as preservers of an historical moment. Or, for example, Elizabeth Barrett Browning's "The Cry of the Children" (1842), an exposé of the human costs of child labor, which led to labor reforms in England. Or, to take another example, Longfellow's verse epic *Evangeline, A Tale of Acady* (1847), which chronicled the story of the expulsion and diaspora of the Acadian people; its huge popularity led to an Acadian cultural renaissance as a quasi-national identity (and even its own flag). Arguably, Ezra Pound's *Cantos* (1915–1962)—that epic poem "containing history"—could also fit the bill. But Charles Reznikoff's *Testimony* (1934) and *Holocaust* (1975) offer an apt, if provisional, point of departure. One of the great "Objectivists"—poets known for their poetry of strict description and unswerving attention to the world, including Louis Zukofsky, George Oppen, Carl Rakosi, and Basil Bunting—Reznikoff worked in a legal publishing house summarizing court records.

This labor led to his major works, *Testimony* (1934, 1979) and *Holocaust* (1975), two book-length docupoems that derive their lines from court proceedings (often highlighting racial crimes) in both the United States and Germany. *Testimony*, originally published as prose in 1934, became a massive two-volume poetic meditation on America that was completed in 1979. For Reznikoff, as for the nineteenth-century balladeers, the story of America unfolded in often shocking acts of violence—acts that demonstrated the dark sides of American life: racism, patriarchal violence, and petty hatreds. (*Holocaust*, similarly, compresses twenty-six volumes of courtroom testimony from the trials of Nazi war criminals in Nuremberg and Jerusalem; Reznikoff self-deprecatingly offers himself as a poetic medium, a secondary witness to the horrors of the Shoah.)

From the beginning of *Testimony*, Reznikoff dramatizes violence and details racial and sexual oppressions with raw understatement. Take for example, "VII: Negroes":

1
One night in April or May,
his daughter saw someone's hand
make the curtain which was drawn tightly across her window
    bulge

and ran to the adjoining room in her night clothes
where he and his son were sitting.
He ran around the house one way
and his son ran the other way
and they found a Negro
under a workbench
within six or eight feet of the window
holding a piece of plank before his face—
begging them not to shoot.

2
The Negro was dead
when the doctors examined him.
They found upon his belly
bruises:
he died, the doctor said, of peritonitis.

The jailer testified that the Negro had been brought to the
     jail
charged with burglary;
but no warrant for his arrest was produced
and the jailer did not know—or tell—
who brought him. The Negro said that a crowd of men
had taken him from a store to the woods
and whipped him
with "a buggy trace."

He was not treated by a doctor, the jailer, or anybody:
just put into the jail and left there to die.
The doctor who saw him first—on a Monday—
did nothing for him
and said that he would not die of his beating;
but he did die of it on Wednesday.[15]

One is struck, first of all, by the silence between the first and
second sections. Like a play in which all the violence happens
offscreen, the poem witnesses both to the initial trespass (a
black man is alleged to have been looking in a white family's
window) to its consequences, written on the body. He dies from
being punched many times in the stomach. The poem's tone
is quiet, almost hushed. It tells us by not telling us so much—

who the killers were, and why the doctor "did nothing for him." Reznikoff's adaptation of spare legalistic language makes the poems vibrate with incommunicability. By setting side by side such episodes, he sutures seemingly disparate situations of American violence, both personal and structural—the black man who was killed after allegedly looking into a white family's window, an Irish woman who disappeared and later was found murdered, going by an alias and running a whorehouse, and the death of a town where the railroad never came—and invites us to reconsider what America is, after all.

Perhaps the great touchstone of documentary poetry is Muriel Rukeyser's "The Book of the Dead" (1938), an unforgettable long poem that tells the stories of mine workers afflicted by silicosis in West Virginia during the late 1920s and early 1930s. Having joined friend Nancy Naumberg, a radical journalist and photographer, for a trip to Gauley Junction, West Virginia, Rukeyser includes court records, first-person interviews, and poetic narrative to create a poem that is evocative of "The Waste Land," if it had been written by Rosa Luxemburg. This poem has, for too long, been one of the least well-known, great poems of the twentieth century. Employing a range of poetic forms (from blues to sonnets), alongside court language, testimonies, and interviews, Rukeyser honors the voices and stories of West Virginia mining families who struggle to make sense of their individual and collective losses. In this labor, Rukeyser becomes a poetic Isis, piecing together the Osirises of Gauley Junction.

Like Reznikoff's *Testimony*, Rukeyser's "The Book of the Dead" is an attempt to include those voices not typically part of poetry, which stand at the margins of American life. It's impossible to summarize the breadth of her poem's achievement in a few short paragraphs. Its ranginess is what distinguishes it from anything that came before and has made it a touchstone for so many other poets. For example, "George Robinson: Blues," a pivotal dramatic monologue from "The Book," sets an African American miner's experience in the blues form; by contrast, "The Disease" takes transcript from a doctor's testimony about silicosis. In contrast to Reznikoff's terse objectivism—which stands at a distance, as in a courtroom—Rukeyser's "Absalom" is dynamic in both form and tone, collaging interview snippets with selections from the Tibetan *Book of the Dead* and actively engaging our imaginative empathy. Here is part of the poem:

> When they took sick, right at the start, I saw a doctor.
> I tried to get Dr. Harless to X-ray the boys.
> He was the only man I had any confidence in,
> the company doctor in the Kopper's mine,
> but he would not see Shirley.
> He did not know where his money was coming from.
> I promised him half if he'd work to get compensation,
> but even then he would not do anything.
> I went on the road and begged the X-ray money,
> the Charleston hospital made the lung pictures,
> he took the case after the pictures were made.
> And two or three doctors said the same thing.
> The youngest boy did not get to go down there with me,
> he lay and said, "Mother, when I die,
> I want you to have them open me up and
> see if that dust killed me.
> Try to get compensation,
> you will not have any way of making your living
> when we are gone,
> and the rest are going too."
>
> *I have gained mastery over my heart*
> *I have gained mastery over my two hands*
> *I have gained mastery over the waters*
> *I have gained mastery over the river.*[16]

In this collage, Rukeyser bears the voice of the mother, who bears the voices of her sons; rather than seeking pity, Rukeyser honors the woman's struggle to care for herself and her children and links it to the "mastery" that the Tibetan text invites of its practitioners. The final lines of "Absalom," spoken by a mother on behalf of her dead son, come to represent Rukeyser's own reclamation project: "He shall not be diminished, never; / I shall give a mouth to my son."[17]

Rukeyser's "The Book of the Dead" is one of the great documentary poems because of its combination of visionary capaciousness and formal technique. It demonstrates a fierce ethical integrity in how it honors a battered people, and yet it reimagines what poetry can do. One can draw a straight line between Rukeyser's poem and practice and the work of C. D. Wright, Mark Nowak, Claudia Rankine, Martha Collins, Susan Tichy, Juliana Spahr, Bhanu Kapil, Erika Meitner, Minnie Bruce Pratt, Rosa Alcalá, Susan Briante, Tyehimba Jess, Solmaz Sharif, Layli Long Soldier, my own writing, and many others. What is haunting about it to me is that Rukeyser never wrote a poem quite like it again; already, poets today are writing not one, but a series of books employing the basic principles evident in "The Book of the Dead." Was it because she'd mastered this new form and decided to move on to other poetic challenges? I have yet to find out.

If Reznikoff and Rukeyser have come to signify a sort of Founding Father and Mother of documentary poetry, I'd nominate Allen Ginsberg as its Court Jester. Specifically, the Ginsberg of "America" (though Ed Sanders's *America: A History in Verse* merits serious consideration as well). While Ginsberg is famous for "Howl" and its earnest anaphoric lamentation for the lost geniuses of his generation, his polyvocal and historically saturated "America" (1956) brings a subversive delight to documentary poetry. In contrast to his oracular poems, Ginsberg's tragicomic "America" queers the news of the repressed 1950s by linking it to the radical zeitgeist of the 1910s–1930s, referencing the Wobblies, Sacco and Vanzetti, and the Scottsboro Boys. In so doing, "America" becomes a monument to its own historical moment, with the mainstream's outsized fears of Communist Russia ("her want to take our cars out of our garages") and his own clownish "beat" resistance to that culture ("It occurs to me that I am America. I am talking to myself again").[18] A poem of rich tonalities and voices, alternately hilarious and angry, "America" feels more liberating than "Howl," and it's a lot more fun to read (and hear):

> America I've given you all and now I'm nothing.
> America two dollars and twentyseven cents January 17, 1956.
> I can't stand my own mind.
> America when will we end the human war?

Go fuck yourself with your atom bomb.
I don't feel good don't bother me.
I won't write my poem till I'm in my right mind.
America when will you be angelic?
When will you take off your clothes?[19]

The famous recording of "America" from 1956 shows Ginsberg at his comic best, intoxicated in all the right ways, and the audience leaning into every word, ready to recognize themselves and laugh. In addition to being a remarkably rich poem that documents its time—albeit in a way that queers or travesties both the 1950s and the 1930s—"America" may well be the closest link poetry has to stand-up comedy, thus satisfying the Horaces of poetry readership, seeking to be delighted far more than instructed.

If we accept Ginsberg's "America" in the halls of documentary poetics, we can widen our sense of what tonalities and approaches might be possible for such poetry; though the dominant tone of documentary poetry has been elegiac, some poets working with "the news" have adopted a tone that melds parody and ferocity. From Flarf and conceptualism to Tyehimba Jess's *OLIO* (2016), which reconstructs the voices of black men and women who participated in minstrel shows, poems employing documentary modes or intervening in investigative ways have ranged far beyond elegiac solidarity and into a field where transgressive comedy and fiery reclamation coexist. With just a small leap, we can include rap-poems like Gil Scott-Heron's "The Revolution Will Not Be Televised" (1970) and Public Enemy's "911 Is a Joke." Chuck D, the mastermind of Public Enemy, the rap group that in the late 1980s stormed onto the popular music scene with *Fear of a Black Planet*, once called rap "the CNN of the ghetto."[20] Sung by comic sidekick Flavor Flav, "911" (1990) called out the miserable performance of emergency services to respond swiftly to calls made from black neighborhoods. Though it's funny, the song is a blistering indictment of the failed social contract. Yet there's plenty of poetry here, in its relentless allusions, both musical and linguistic; when Flav compares the loss of limbs to "compilation,"[21] he uses the metaphors of the music industry to lay bare the brute economics of emergency medical treatment. I can't help but think of Whitman's "Song of Myself," in which the poet juxtaposes the selling of a quadroon girl to the amputation of a diseased limb that "drops horribly in a pail."[22] For Whitman, as for Flav, black people have been treated as expendable appendages. Whitman's juxtaposition, it seems to me, participates or at least anticipates the kinds of fierce suturing of the investigative poem.

Because documentary poetry has some roots in the ballad tradition, then we should not ignore how popular music has contributed to this poetic tradition. Consider the recent Nobel Prize for Literature awardee, Bob Dylan. Early Dylan is rife with acerbic and newsworthy topical songs that captured the racial and class contradictions of life during the years of unprecedented prosperity after the Second World War. Harry Smith's famous *Anthology of American Folk Music* (1952), one of Dylan's seminal influences, contains a record of ballads that demonstrate the tradition of the balladeer who adapts lurid news stories, such as the sinking of the Titanic ("When That Great Ship Went Down") or the assassination of a President ("Charles Guiteau"),[23] telling them from an outsider's point of view. The ballad, after all, has long been admitted into the poetry canon, from ballad songs like "Barbara Allen" to the hymn-based poems of Emily Dickinson.

Dylan's "The Lonesome Death of Hattie Carroll" (1964) departs from some of the strictures of the poetic form, but its use of rhyme and compressed storytelling places it within this tradition. It tells the story of politically connected and wealthy William Zantzinger's killing of a 51-year-old black woman, Hattie Carroll, and his subsequent sentence of six months in jail.[24] The sentence came in August 1963, and just two months later, Dylan had recorded the song and would play it regularly during live shows and on television. Bringing to light not only the gruesome story but also the sentimentalizing coverage of the event in the mass media ("now ain't the time for your tears"),[25] Dylan intervened in the case in a way he would repeat years later when he took on the case of Rubin "Hurricane" Carter in "Hurricane"—a song whose selective shaping of the events of a murder has been as debated almost as much as the case itself.

Dylan is one of a whole raft of lyricists whose work extends and humanizes the news. It's funny for me to remember that I first learned about Apartheid from Peter Gabriel's "Biko" (1980), about U.S. foreign policy in Latin America from U2's "Bullet the Blue Sky" (1987), and about the Mothers of the Disappeared from Sting's "They Dance Alone" (1988). Consider, for example, how Mos Def's "New World Water" (1999) lays bare the connection between global climate change and the commodification of water:

Tell your crew use the H2 in wise amounts since
It's the New World Water; and every drop counts
You can laugh and take it as a joke if you wanna
But it don't rain for four weeks some summers
And it's about to get real wild in the half
You be buying Evian just to take a fuckin bath[26]

In light of the contamination of Flint's public water supply in 2014, in which people have been exposed to massive lead poisoning and compelled to shower with bottled water, Mos Def's song has been prophetic. In an age of global climate change, the push to privatize drinking water threatens to increase inequality, while lining the pockets of the wealthy:

Cause foreign-based companies go and get greedy
The type of cats who pollute the whole shore line
Have it purified, sell it for a dollar twenty-five
Now the world is drinkin it
Your moms, wife, and baby girl is drinkin it
Up north and down south is drinkin it
You should just have to go to your sink for it
The cash registers is goin "cha-chink!" for it
Fluorocarbons and monoxide
Got the fish lookin cockeyed
Used to be free now it cost you a fee
Cause it's all about gettin that cash (money)[27]

Documentary poetry is not merely an American phenomenon; examples of documentary poetics abound throughout the globe, part of a tool kit of avant-garde and radical poetic practices to recover and restore repressed voices, stories, and histories from the scrubbed public records of the powerful. A Jesuit priest and former minister of culture after the Sandinista Revolution, Ernesto Cardenal wrote the title poem to *Zero Hour and Other Documentary Poems* (1980) in the mid-1950s to dramatize the Nicaraguan struggle for economic and political independence from the United States and the eventual assassination of revolutionary Nicaraguan guerrilla Carlos Sandino. Other poems in this collection, inspired by Pablo Neruda's *Canto General* (itself another touchstone of documentary poetry), chronicle the 1979 revolution as it is happening—an ecstatic, though not always successful, revolutionary poetry. This moment, from the poem "Zero Hour," gives us a broad economic analysis of the situation on the ground for *campesinos* during the Somoza regime:

> And the farmers are put in jail for not selling at 30 cents
> and their bananas are slashed with bayonets
> and the Mexican Trader Steamship sinks with their barges
>   on them
> and the strikers are cowed with bullets.
> (And the Nicaraguan congressmen are invited to a garden
>   party.)
> But the black worker has seven children.
> And what can you do? You've got to eat,
> And you've got to accept what they offer to pay.[28]

Some have noted how Cardenal's poetry detailing the past served a critical historiographical function in a society where dissent was suppressed; some of the poems written in the heat of the revolution occasionally lapse into an uncritical celebration of all done in the name of revolution. Translator Robert Pring-Mill, who first called Cardenal's poetry "documentary," notes that these poems use filmic techniques such as "crosscutting, accelerated montage, or flash frames . . . [which] is aimed at helping to shape the future—involving the reader in the poetic process in order to provoke him into full political commitment."[29] As his readers put together the fragments of history, they participate in its telling and offer their own versions of where their common future might lead.

Outside the United States, poets such as Neruda and Cardenal, Aimé Cesáire and Mahmoud Darwish, documented national struggles against colonialism in their poetry, while inside, poets such as Peter Dale Scott, Denise Levertov, June Jordan, and H. L. Hix made visible the often-invisible extension of American empire. Documentary poetry as anti-imperialist, anti-war practice emerged with ferocity in the late 1960s, with notable books such as Daniel Berrigan's dramatic trial-poem *The Trial of the Catonsville Nine* (1970), Robert Bly's *The Teeth-Mother Naked at Last* (1970), Levertov's *To Stay Alive* (1971), and John Balaban's *After Our War* (1974), tracing the political and psychic dimensions of war resistance in the United States, a movement derided and misrepresented by mass media.

When literature scholar Tracy Ware argued that "*Coming to Jakarta* is in a way the long poem that [Noam] Chomsky never wrote,"[30] he captured the essentially radical nature of Peter Dale Scott's odd and compelling epic poem, published in 1989. Yet Chomsky, the linguistic and political anarchist known for his unrufflable rationalism, never demonstrates the subjective terror that Scott summons in this nerve-bundled recounting of the poet's heady encounters with international political intrigue.

In this poem, Scott records the process of uncovering his personal, familial, and political relationships to the subterranean machinations of the CIA in the 1960s. The first in a trilogy of long poems, it tells the previously untold history of CIA involvement in Indonesia, particularly during the 1965 massacre of half of a million people. Scott turns to poetry partly because no one will publish an unexpurgated version of the CIA's role in Indonesia and elsewhere during the Cold War. Poetry, for Scott, flies under the radar of the censoring apparatus still in place in prose.

xvii

And now East Timor
    where in 1977
   the Indonesian minister admits

perhaps 80,000 might have been killed

        that is to say one person out of eight
    by his own government's paracommandos

these gentle midnight faces
        the beetles which crowd their eyes
    From 1975 to 1977

the New York Times index
        entries for East Timor
    dropped from six columns

to five lines[31]

Though the poem occasionally lapses into (or perhaps thrives upon) conspiracy theories, it also embodies how poetry can become both a medium for and matrix of unspoken histories. Yet this work also raises an unresolved and little-discussed implication of investigative poetics—the question of facticity itself. In other words, investigative poems such as Scott's or, more infamously, Amiri Baraka's "Somebody Killed America"—which, among its long catalogue of Western imperial depredation, also included an anti-Semitic rumor about Israeli foreknowledge of 9/11—compel readers to question the very truthfulness of the work as a whole, or whether the poem's ultimate truth is not as simple as a lesson in Western imperialism, but rather, as I have suggested elsewhere, also a dramatic rendering of the pitfalls of conspiracy thinking.

Though Levertov's *To Stay Alive* marked her most intense engagement with documentary poetry, her "News Report, September 1991: U.S. Buried Iraqi Soldiers Alive in Gulf War" collages a back page journalistic account of the U.S. mass "burial" of Iraqi soldiers.[32] Levertov performs a "cut-up" of the original article, fragmenting its language to render the traumatic effects of a U.S. military operation, which involved bulldozing trenches during Operation Desert Storm, thus burying alive the Iraqi soldiers inside:

"His force buried
about six hundred

and fifty
in a thinner line
of trenches."
"People's arms
sticking out."
"Every American
inside."
"The juggernaut."[33]

Repeating and juxtaposing the words of the U.S. military spokesmen, the poet highlights the limited media access to the war (and hence, the impossibility of non-military witness), and underlines the war's connections to capitalism. Phrases like "carefully planned and/rehearsed" or "the tactic was designed" easily could have emerged from a corporate board meeting.[34] The terrible limit of corporate thinking is captured in Colonel Moreno's assertion that the U.S. burial of Iraqis was justifiable because the possibility of American casualties while burying Iraqi bodies individually is not "cost-effective."[35]

June Jordan's multi-sectioned "The Bombing of Baghdad" (1997) ranges from a catalogue of the bombing to the lovers' bed to an address to a leap to Native American history—as if to mark the trajectory of the war in a longer history of oppression, one which attempts to reach into our very bedrooms. The poem's first section begins with a litany that pummels the audience with the particular human catastrophe of a war that was largely unrepresented in mass media, despite its being the first simulcast war:

> began and did not terminate for 42 days
> and 42 nights relentless minute after minute
> more than 100,000 times
> we bombed Iraq we bombed Baghdad
> we bombed Basra/we bombed military
> installations we bombed the National Museum
> we bombed schools we bombed air raid
> shelters we bombed water we bombed
> electricity we bombed hospitals we
> bombed streets we bombed highways
> we bombed everything that moved/we

bombed Baghdad
a city of 5.5 million human beings.[36]

In contrast to the triumphalist media reports of the time, Jordan's poem acts as an alternative news source, faithfully documenting the extent of the bombing—which attacked basic infrastructure in ways from which Iraq could not recover, particularly during the period of economic sanctions. Further, her employment of the "we"—which U.S. news outlets used to describe the lack of distance between the military effort, the media, and its American audience—now cuts back against us, rendering our complicity visible, admonishing us and herself.

Ten years later, in *God Bless* (2007), H. L. Hix composes a series of mathematically formal poems culled from speeches, executive orders, and other public statements of George W. Bush, then interleaves them with poems based on the letters and speeches of Osama bin Laden. The poems comically, and frighteningly, render Bush's language into forms as elaborate and exotic as the sestina and the ghazal. By taking these men at their word—literally and figuratively—Hix demonstrates how aesthetic attention becomes a kind of ethical and political attention, a close reading of the first order. In "September 2001," Hix culls from Bush's speeches during that pivotal month to create the following:

Our country will . . . not be cowed by terrorists,
by people who don't share the same values we share.
Those responsible for these cowardly acts
hate our values; they hate what America stands for.
We can't let terrorism dictate our course of action.
We're a nation that has fabulous values:
as a nation of good folks, we're going to hunt them down,
and we're going to find them, and . . . bring them to justice.
Either you are with us, or you are with the terrorists.
They're flat evil. They have no justification.
There is universal support for what we intend.
Americans are asking: What is expected of us?
I ask you to live your lives, and hug your children.
Go back to work. Get down to Disney World.[37]

Rather than merely deriding the president, selectively quoting malapropisms, Hix distills his representative language. And what does it mean to have a president voiced into sonnets? What does it mean not only for the president, but also for the sonnet? In contrast to *Pieces of Intelligence*, a book that works the language of Donald Rumsfeld into poetry, Hix's poems do not extend or ironize political rhetoric. On the contrary, as Susan Schultz has written, "Rumsfeld wants to get people off his scent so he can do things. [Poetry] is the scent, you could say—it's really trying to get you deep into a cultural moment or political moment, or just into how language works."[38] Harvey Hix does precisely that—he brings us more fully into the political moment and shows how language is being used, and misused, in the War on Terror.

A document of close listening, *God Bless* aptly demonstrates the profound lack of listening at the heart of the Bush administration's decision-making process—in ironic contrast to bin Laden's obsessive study and reply to U.S. policy. Take, for example, bin Laden's reply to the events of 9/11: "Again and again he claims to know our reason, / and tells you we attacked because we hate freedom. / *Perhaps he can tell us why we did not attack Sweden.*"[39] In contrast to Bush's sound-bite speeches, bin Laden's speeches used a formal rhetoric and richly complex argumentation that was almost impossible to form into poems. It is terrifying to realize that, despite bin Laden's obvious deficiencies—his anti-Semitism, his fundamentalism, his selective reading of history—his arguments have a logic that our own president's frequently lacks. In Hix's rendering, *God Bless* becomes a kind of history lesson, a way of reading into the archive and thus extending the archive into poetry, poetry that works to extend the document.

Documentary poets have also opened up ways of seeing and listening to those who have experienced oppression in the United States due to race, gender, and class. Claudia Rankine's *Don't Let Me Be Lonely* (2004) and *Citizen* (2014) have been acclaimed, rightfully, for their granular explorations of racism—from microaggressions to police brutality—including the well-known page in *Citizen* that, with each new printing of the book, continues to add the names of black people killed at the hands of police. Similarly, and worthy of further attention, Martha Collins' *Blue Front* (2006)—the first of a trilogy of documentary poetry books, including *White Papers* (2012) and *Admit One* (2016), meditating on race—engages in an act of poetic historiography, in which she reconstructs her father's experience, who, as a five-year-old, witnessed the lynching of a black man in the small town of Cairo, Illinois. Collins sets in motion the contradictory and overlapping accounts of what happened on that fateful day to probe the difficulty of telling the story of traumatic events.

C. D. Wright's *One Big Self* (2006) culls statements and stories from her time interviewing inmates with photographer Deborah Luster in three prisons in Louisiana, following in the tradition of Muriel Rukeyser's trip to Gauley Junction with photographer Nancy Naumberg. Wright juggles these voices and images in ways that create "one big self" that contains author, reader, prisoner, and the prison industrial complex.

Though moments of the book quote and collage prisoner's voices, Wright's work is not primarily composed of them. Certain moments pepper the fabric of the work, as when a prisoner confesses to Wright, "The last time you was here I had a headful of bees."[40] The language of the prisoners is not embodied but rather floats, hauntingly, among the language of everything and everyone else; the One Big Self of the title is not necessarily the mystic's dream of communion with all souls but the disorienting and painful fragments of incomplete selves, broken into cells.

In "Dialing Dungeons for Dollars," an explicitly "documentary" section, Wright indicts the capitalism profit-making embedded in the criminal justice system, which Michelle Alexander famously termed "the New Jim Crow": "The good news is: / Corrections Corporation of America increased its inmate mandays by / 12% From 15.1 million in 1998 to 16.9 million in 1999 A manday is one / inmate held for one day for which the company bills government a *per* / *diem* The increase in mandays in 1999 led to a 19% increase in CCA's / revenues for the year to $787 million."[41] Wright's "good news" is, of course, the opposite of good news except for CCA shareholders. She documents here not only the profit margin but also the way a new Orwellian language is created by the prison industrial complex, where profits require prisoners and their lives, counted in "mandays."

In "Dear Prisoner," Wright addresses the prisoners themselves as a collective subject, trying to bridge the abyss between their reality and hers, admitting:

> I too love. Faces. Hands. The circumference
> Of the oaks. I confess. To nothing
> You could use. In a court of law. I found.
> That sickly sweet ambrosia of hope. Unmendable
> Seine of sadness. Experience taken away.
> From you. I would open. The mystery
> Of your birth. To you. I know. We can
> Change. Knowing. Full well. Knowing.

> It is not enough.[42]

Wright's use of punctuation chops the sentences into broken units, as if to suggest the pressure of outside forces, the fact of this distance between her and the prisoners embodied by these interruptive periods. Despite the particularity of the prisoner's portraits taken by Naumberg, Wright senses her distance from these lives, and that all her well-meaning attempts to bring those faces and hands and lives to the outside world is blocked by systems and institutions larger than the arts. She knows "it is not enough," but that doesn't stop her from the work of showing what cannot be shown, of speaking what cannot be spoken. Throughout *One Big Self*, Wright's documentary poetics ride the ambiguity of that enjambment of the second to third lines—that her poetry is between a "nothing" and a something that could be used. Their power comes from their negotiation between the language of evidence and the language of transcendence. She would continue to explore the possibilities of documentary writing in *Rising, Falling, and Hovering* (2008) and explicitly in *One with Others* (2011).

With Wright's death in 2016, Mark Nowak—whose *Shut Up Shut Down* (2004) and *Coal Mountain Elementary* (2009) became instant classics for their exploration of working class lives facing capitalist depredation at home and abroad—has become the contemporary documentary poet whose efforts have worked to overcome the divide that Wright's work brings to light, between her own witness and the lives of others. *Shut Up Shut Down* embodies, on the level of form, the brutal speed by which global neoliberalism has gutted whole ways of life in the industrial Rust Belt; the title intimates how the shuttering of good union jobs has devastated a whole generation of working people, stealing not only the livelihoods but their very ability to speak their truth. In *Shut Up Shut Down*, Nowak's poems work through active jump-cutting or sampling, braiding three voices or discourses. Take this example from "Capitalization," a long poem braiding the voices of workers, news reports of the 1981 Air Traffic Controllers (PATCO) strike, and grammatical rules for capitalization:

> **In spite of those tough times,**
> **There was a feeling of solidarity.**
> **If a family was put out of their house,**
> **People would gather there to stop the eviction.**
> *As the "host," he occupied a more defensible position.*
> *It was Reagan who ended each show*
> *With the famous slogan,*
> *"Here at General Electric,*
> *Progress is our most important product."*
> **When gas and electricity were shut off,**
> **Unemployed workers would go around**
> **And turn them back on.**
> Do not capitalize the following
> When they stand alone: judge, justice
> Capitalize President . . .[43]

Throughout, as if to underscore his solidarity, Nowak bolds the voice of the laborer and italicizes the ironically placed news report. Only the grammar rules appear in normal type-face. In this passage, the laborer recalls a time of collective effort, where people pitched in and helped each other through hard times. This is contrasted with the dazzle of Reagan on television, touting the "progress" of General Electric, the same company shutting off the lights of workers who have fallen on tough times.

Perhaps even more important than his formidably experimental work, Nowak's cultivation of audience (or rather, rethinking what audience actually might mean) has been his most noteworthy achievement. After seeing his first book receive attention only from poets, he went about "consciously attempt[ing] to construct a new audience, a new social space, for the potential reception of [his] work and other new works that might emerge in this vein."[44] One poem, the verse play "Francine Michalek Drives Bread," Nowak recounts, "premiered at UAW Local 879 union hall across the street from the Ford plant in St. Paul. The audience, uniquely, was split half-and-half between people from the literary community (and those split evenly among poetry and theater people) and workers from the Ford plant along with activists from various unions."[45] Nowak found ways of reading his work for labor audiences, in the midst of union fundraising, unionizing, and striking; for labor radio shows; and in publications that specialize in labor.

If *Shut Up Shut Down* initiated that practice, it became even more explicit when *Coal Mountain Elementary*—a book-length dramatic poem setting the Sago Mine disaster, Chinese mining reports, photographs by Nowak and Ian Teh, and elementary school lesson plans created by the U.S. coal industry—was staged in the Boilerhouse Theater at Davis & Elkins College in 2009, just miles from where the Sago mine disaster had occurred; the active involvement of people in the community who experienced the disaster has pointed toward his ongoing work doing The Worker Writers School, about which I'll say more below. While *Shut Up* is more "poetic" in its treatment of language, the line, and syntax, *Coal Mountain Elementary* is, in some sense, more "dramatic" or even "novelistic"—particularly in the way that the whole book could be read as a single work broken into chapters, in which the page itself is a unit of measure. Nowak's poetic trajectory has moved from the lyric (in his first book, *Revenants*) to the narrative, polyvocal, intertextual, and multimedia.

Documentary poems are not meant to be merely *objets d'art*. They are signals in the dark, compilations of the possible. For Craig Santos Perez, documentary poetics is "the act of weaving history, poetry, myths, legends, tradition, tale, record, anecdote (certainly more) into something that both amplifies each of them while it also contributes something new to a collective continuance."[46] The labor of documentary poetry moves toward the articulation of a collectivity with its own language, its own stories. And now, new generations of documentary poetry have emerged, conscious of this sudden tradition. My reading of Jordan, Rukeyser, Nowak, and Jen Bervin, for example, informed how I approached the Abu Ghraib prison scandal in *Sand Opera*. The legacy of Jordan's melding of fiery authoritativeness and vulnerability undergirds Solmaz Sharif's *Look* (2016), just as the deconstruction of legal texts in M. Nourbese Philip's *Zong!* (2008) inspires Layli Long Soldier's *WHEREAS* (2016), as it writes back to the 2010 apology by the U.S. government for its violent treatment of native people. And these two poets, both of whom employ the legal term "whereas," should be read alongside each other and within documentary poetics, obsessed as it is with the way power camouflages itself in the language of law.

I need to return to Mark Nowak's work one last time. Nowak actually dislikes the term documentary poetry, preferring Langston Hughes's "social poetry." Rather than writing about his own personal struggles, Hughes chose to write about the struggle of ordinary people for a good life amid racial and economic oppression. In his essay on social poetry, Hughes noted that this radical practice must be powerful, because "when poems stop talking about the moon and begin to mention poverty, trade unions, color lines, and colonies, somebody tells the police."[47] Nowak's unease about the very term "documentary poetry" parallels his own work since the publication of *Shut Up Shut Down* and *Coal Mountain Elementary*. Despite the critical success of these books, Nowak always saw his work as a departure point for empowering, rather than representing, others and othered voices. Leaping from his consideration of the struggle of industrial workers in *Shut Up Shut Down*, Nowak conducted workshops with autoworkers from Ford plants in Detroit and South Africa. Since then, in recent projects, and in his Worker Writers School, rather than merely representing the struggle of domestic workers in his own writing, he has conducted workshops with domestic workers and gathered their poems as part of an international campaign to create a domestic worker bill of rights. According to Nowak, "these workshops create a space for participants to re-imagine their working lives, nurture new literary voices directly from the global working class, and produce new tactics and imagine new futures for working class social change."[48] Nowak's work revisions the basic idea of the poem and the writing workshop for the masses of people who have been excluded both from literature and from creative writing; he's the closest we have to a Wobbly (IWW) poet, a true radical culture worker.

Inspired by Nowak and others, Anthony Shoplik, Zachary Thomas, Rachel Schratz, Michalena Mezzopera, and I began a poetry workshop program at Cleveland's Juvenile Detention Center in 2016, called JCU Writers in Residence. On the first day, after playing basketball with about a dozen African American teenagers, we repaired to the library and talked about Mos Def's "Umi Says" and Gwendolyn Brooks' "Mother to Son," writing about advice we'd been given and what we'd give to siblings or to our younger selves. I can't tell you how beautiful it was to be in their quiet as they worked on their lines, and then listened to them share them, one after another. The students gave them a survey at the end, and the teens said they wanted more, so we've begun a full-time program. What they said about poetry restored my faith in the possibilities of the art: "Helped me to express myself." "Allowed me to get stuff off my chest." "I learned something new about myself." "Let me know that no matter what happened, there's always another chance." "Helped us bond like family." "I felt like I had a family again."[49] Part of our program will be education about the prison-industrial complex, and I'm hoping they will be empowered to use their voices to tell their experiences and also to transform the systems in which they find themselves.

We need to ask ourselves, in our own institutions and structures of power: Are we merely self-replicating, or are we building something new? Are we and our poetry assisting in the perpetuation of unjust systems? Has it become robotic assembly-line production? Does it offer, in its partial sight, some way forward through the eclipse-dark of our contemporary moment? As Paul Goodman invited activists in the last century: "Suppose you had the Revolution you are talking and dreaming about. Suppose your side had won, and you had the kind of society that you wanted . . . how would you live, you personally, in that society? Start living that way now."[50]

In the introduction to *Tracking/Teaching*, Joe Harrington proposes that "the test of any documentary/historical/investigative poetry" is whether it "ends up teaching the new reading publics things that they did not know already."[51] Certainly, documentary poetry offers us not only a new method of poetry, and not only a new way of telling history, but also a new way of making history. The aim of making poetry to make change, to make history, is what makes Nowak's work most radical and most daring, moving into the realm where knowing is a kind of collective being and doing. In the end, I am not concerned with defining or guarding the borders of documentary poetry, or marketing it as an exciting subgenre to teach young poets. Our *telos* as poets should not be to preserve the sanctity or avant-garde credentials of documentary poetry but to transform and be transformed by the radical possibilities of creating spaces for poems to happen, by widening the idea of authorship beyond the academy, finding poetry where it always existed: in the mouths of those who have been shut up and shut down, from the pens of those whose lives have been written out of History, and must make their own.

Notes

1. Thanks to Kazim Ali, David Baker, Marilyn Hacker, and Laura Wetherington for their useful comments on this version of the essay, which quotes generously from the original essay "From Reznikoff to Public Enemy" and also from my afterword to Joe Harrington's "Tracking/Teaching: On Documentary Poetics" (Essay Press).

2. William Carlos Williams, "Asphodel, That Greeny Flower," in *Journey to Love* (New York: Random House, 1955).

3. Ibid.

4. Camille T. Dungy and Adrian Matejka, "Full of Many Stars: Pushing Past (and Pushing the Past into) the Heliocentric Poem," in *Tracking/Teaching: On Documentary Poetics*, curated by Joseph Harrington (Essay Press, 2015).

5. Craig Santos Perez and Donovan Kūhiō Colleps, "Two Pacific Decolonial Docu-Poets Walk into a Tiki Bar," in *Tracking/Teaching: On Documentary Poetics*, curated by Joseph Harrington (Essay Press, 2015), 4.

6. Dungy and Matejka, "Full of Many Stars," 31.

7. Kaia Sand and Allison Cobb, "A Small Encyclopedia of Life, Death & Other Investigations," in *Tracking/Teaching: On Documentary Poetics*, curated by Joseph Harrington (Essay Press, 2015), 50.

8. Kenneth Goldsmith, "The Body of Michael Brown" (poem pre-

sented at Interrupt 3 conference, Granoff Center for the Creative Arts, Brown University, March 12–15, 2015).

9. Rin Johnson, "On Hearing a White Man Co-opt the Body of Michael Brown," *Hyperallergic,* March 20, 2015, http://hyperallergic.com/192628/on-hearing-a-white-man-co-opt-the-body-of-michael-brown/

10. Gayatri Spivak, "Can the Subaltern Speak?" *Wedge* 7/8 (Winter/Spring 1985).

11. James Baldwin, *The Fire Next Time* (New York: Dial Press, 1963), quoted in *Collected Essays,* vol. 2 (Ann Arbor: University of Michigan Press, 1998), 333.

12. Howard Zinn, preface to *Twentieth Century: A People's History* (New York: HarperCollins, 1980), x.

13. Kaia Sand and Allison Cobb, "A Small Encyclopedia," 50.

14. Mark Nowak, *Shut Up Shut Down: Poems* (Minneapolis: Coffee House Press, 2004), 2.

15. Charles Reznikoff, *Testimony* (New York: The Objectivist Press, 1934), quoted in *Testimony: The United States, 1885–1915* (Santa Rosa: Black Sparrow Press, 1978), 40.

16. Muriel Rukeyser, "The Book of the Dead," in *U.S. 1* (New York: Covici-Friede, 1938), quoted in *Out of Silence: Selected Poems* by Muriel Rukeyser, ed. Kate Daniels (Illinois: Triquarterly Books/Northwestern, 1994), 19.

17. Ibid., 20.

18. Allen Ginsberg, "America," in *Howl and Other Poems* (San Francisco: City Lights Books, 1955), 41.

19. Ibid.

20. Chuck D quoted in Teresa Wiltz, "It's Still a Party, but Hip-Hop Is Testing Political Waters," *Los Angeles Times,* June 28, 2002.

21. Flavor Flav, Public Enemy, "911 Is a Joke," in *Fear of a Black Planet,* compact disc, Def Jam Recordings, 1990.

22. Walt Whitman, "Song of Myself," in *Leaves of Grass* (New York: Dover Editions, 1855), 30.

23. Harry Smith, *Anthology of American Folk Music,* vinyl, Folkways Records, 1952.

24. Bob Dylan, "The Lonesome Death of Hattie Carroll," in *The Times They Are a-Changin',* vinyl, Columbia Records, 1964.

25. Ibid.

26. Mos Def, "New World Water," in *Black on Both Sides,* compact disc, Rawkus Records, 1999.

27. Ibid.

28. Ernesto Cardenal, "Zero Hour," in *Zero Hour and Other Documentary Poems,* trans. Robert Pring-Mill (New York: New Directions, 1980), 3.

29. Ibid, ix.

30. Tracy Ware, "Shifting Sand of a Son's Radical Faith in Peter Dale Scott's *Coming to Jakarta: A Poem about Terror*," *University of Toronto Quarterly* 7.4 (2002), doi: 10.3138/utq.71.4.827.

31. Peter Dale Scott, *Coming to Jakarta: A Poem about Terror* (New York: New Directions, 1988), 140.

32. Denise Levertov, "News Report, September 1991: U.S. Buried Iraqi Soldiers Alive in Gulf War," in *Evening Train* (New York: New Directions, 1992), 82.

33. Ibid.

34. Ibid.

35. Ibid.

36. June Jordan, "The Bombing of Baghdad," in *Kissing God Goodbye: Poems 1991–1997* (Norwell: Anchor Books, 1997), quoted in "The Bombing of Baghdad," http://www.junejordan.net/the-bombing-of-baghdad.html

37. H. L. Hix, *God Bless: A Political/Poetical Discourse* (Wilkes-Barre, PA: Etruscan, 2007), 21.

38. Christine Thomas, ed., "What I'm Reading: Susan Schultz," *The Honolulu Weekly*, May 20, 2007, accessed August 27, 2010, http://www.tinfishpress.com/about_us/advertiser/index.html?AID=2007705200356

39. H. L. Hix, op. cit., 23.

40. C. D. Wright, *One Big Self* (Port Townsend, WA: Copper Canyon, 2007), 5.

41. Ibid., 28.

42. Ibid., 42.

43. Mark Nowak, *Shut Up Shut Down* (St. Paul, MN: Coffee House Press, 2004), 36.

44. Mark Nowak, interviewed by Philip Metres, "Poetry as Social Practice in the First Person Plural: A Dialogue on Documentary Poetics," *Iowa Journal of Cultural Studies* 12 (2010), 14, http://ir.uiowa.edu/ijcs/vol12/iss1/3

45. Ibid.

46. Ibid., 4.

47. Langston Hughes, "My Adventures as a Social Poet," *Phylon* 8.3 (1947), 205.

48. "Worker Writers School Collaboration," The Ed Factory, LLC, https://theedfactory.org/worker-writers-school/

49. Informal anonymous survey, taken November 2016.

50. Paul Goodman, quoted in Rebecca Solnit, *Hope in the Dark* (Chicago: Haymarket Books, 2016), xxiv.

51. *Tracking/Teaching: On Documentary Poetics* (Essay Press, 2015), v.

"We Build a World"

War Resistance Poetry in/as the First Person Plural

> Let us suppose that we had carried out production as human beings. . . . I would have been for you the *mediator* between you and the species, and therefore would become recognised and felt by yourself as a completion of your own essential nature and as a necessary part of yourself, and consequently would know myself to be confirmed both in your thought and your love. . . . In the individual expression of my life I would have directly created your expression of your life, and therefore in my individual activity I would have directly *confirmed* and *realised* my true nature, my *human* nature, my *communal* nature.
>
> —Karl Marx[1]

> "SOCIAL SCULPTURE—how we mold and shape the world in which we live: SCULPTURE AS AN EVOLUTIONARY PROCESS; EVERYONE AN ARTIST."
>
> —Joseph Beuys[2]

If everyone is indeed an artist, as avant-gardist Joseph Beuys once proposed, and our lives on some level are works of art, then socially active poets who engage in readings, teach workshops, and write books of poetry have another vital critical role: coaxing others who are not traditionally hailed to *realize* (in both senses, to become aware of and to actualize) their own labors of making as art—*poesis* being that great making—and seeing how poetry itself changes when these "others" create it. In the process, the poet as mediator, as listener, as shaper, as chronicler, might realize her "true nature," as Marx puts it, her "communal nature."

I received an email from Alex Chambers, a poet and activist, thanking me for my Poetry Foundation piece on documentary poetry, "From Reznikoff to Public Enemy," noting that he included it in his prison poetry workshop. He noted one particularly powerful poem emerged from the participants in response to the possibilities of documentary poetry. Overall, though, Chambers found that the prisoners were more drawn to the first person lyric than to the operations of documentary poetics—partly because of their perceived notions about what poetry is, and partly because the poetry of lyric provided the aura of agency and the technology of voice that the prisoners felt that they so lacked.

Chambers must have felt a little disappointed, knowing that documentary poetry offers possibilities that the expressivist lyric does not; anyone who has taught poetry has, from time to time, felt that acutely painful chasm between one's own pleasures in texts and the students' pleasures. Yet if we poets are interested in poetry as a mode of social change, as an operation of social and symbolic action, and as a medium by which individuals and communities can dialogue with each other and the world, then we must be attuned to the needs and goals of the communities with which they work. This is not to say that we must abandon our principles and pleasures in poetry; on the contrary, since poetry is like bread to us, we must continue to eat, to live. But if we are to participate in the poetics of a community, we must find what will feed our fellow members. To pivot the metaphor slightly, we must be the ears of the movements in which we find ourselves, as much as the mouths.

In concert with the publication of *Behind the Lines*, I began a blog to update and extend the concerns of the book, since I was aware the heavily academic discourse occasionally makes the prose difficult. When University of Iowa Press chose to publish the book only in hardcover edition, I began to look for ways to dialogue with peace movement activists more directly, since I feared that my call to liberate poems would be itself imprisoned in libraries.

The Poetics of the Collective
and the Collective Poem

In November 2009, the National War Tax Resistance Coordinating Committee held their annual meeting in a church in Cleveland; one of their members asked me to join and do a poetry reading, or something that might be a warm-up to the weekend program. Though I am not a war tax resister, I have long supported national legislation to create a Department of Peace and to reduce war and "defense" spending.

Instead of doing a traditional poetry reading, which could have led easily to a static Poet as Authority and Audience as Passive Recipient, I had an opportunity to put my theory into action, and engage the praxis that I have been advocating for years. I came up with a writing exercise that would produce a co-authored "chorale," a collective poem that would reflect both the diversity of experiences and viewpoints of the participants, as well as their unity in resisting war and working for a more just and peaceful world.

I began by reading two poems from the anthology *Come Together: Imagine Peace*. "The Story So Far" by Shara McCallum, and "Jerusalem" by Naomi Shihab Nye. I chose them because I thought they had a relatively approachable theme and use of language, and I noted to the participants the ways in which each poem offers us a particular vision of the world—its deserts of violence and its oases of peace. In "The Story So Far," McCallum witnesses to the brutality of human beings toward one another, a world in which there is nothing that we have not done to each other.

The Story So Far

To choose a song for sacrifice
the war continues:

as four thousand years
Isaac and Ishmael still clamouring for God's ear.

In the light of day's end, in a warehouse in Rwanda,
a Hutu foreman hovers over one of his workers,

a pregnant Tutsi woman. This ordinary man
with a wife, children of his own,

will disembowel her. Not a stranger
but this woman he knows. To learn

as later, in his defense, he will confess—
what the inside of a Tutsi woman is like.

On the radio, a young woman recounts her tale
of the Cambodia killing fields:

rice paddies, thatched hut where she plays,
men coming for her father first,

her mother orphaning her so she might survive.
This child eating crickets and coal to stay alive.

Butterflies by the hundreds alight on her face,
cover each inch of skin, their furred wings

opening and closing
against her eyelids, lips and cheeks.

Told in any language—the parables of suffering,
the fractured syllables of loss,

the space in the back of a throat
still longing to sound the names of God.[3]

I noted briefly the horrible power of these particular images of
violence, and how the poet's task is the human task of finding
"the space in the back of the throat." The great ambiguity at
the end of the poem does not resolve whether the "longing to
sound the names of God" is a fundamentally transformative and
humane act of reclamation, or one which is destined to fall into
the same "story so far" (cf. the competition between Ishmael
and Isaac "for God's ear).

In the second poem, "Jerusalem," Naomi Shihab Nye juxtaposes images of brokenness and pain with ones of transformative magic, art, and faith; in particular, I wanted to demonstrate
how the poet shows us that peace is as natural and human as
violence may be:

Jerusalem

"Let's be the same wound if we must bleed.
Let's fight side by side, even if the enemy
is ourselves: I am yours, you are mine."
   —Tommy Olofsson, Sweden

I'm not interested in
who suffered the most.
I'm interested in
people getting over it.

Once when my father was a boy
a stone hit him on the head.
Hair would never grow there.
Our fingers found the tender spot
and its riddles: the boy who has fallen
stands up. A bucket of pears
in his mother's doorway welcomes him home.
The pears are not crying.
Lately his friend who threw the stone
says he was aiming at a bird.
And my father starts growing wings.

Each carries a tender spot:
something our lives forgot to give us.
A man builds a house and says,
"I am native now."
A woman speaks to a tree in place
of her son. And olives come.
A child's poem says,
"I don't like wars,
they end up with monuments."
He's painting a bird with wings
wide enough to cover two roofs at once.

Why are we so monumentally slow?
Soldiers stalk a pharmacy:
Big guns, little pills.
If you tilt your head just slightly
it's ridiculous.

There's a place in this brain
where hate won't grow.
I touch its riddles: wind and seeds.
Something pokes us as we sleep.

It's late but everything comes next.[4]

I then invited them to do two free-writes, in five-minute incre-
ments:

1. Describe an image or moment of rupture or violence that
you experienced or witnessed that has always stayed with you,
that you carry with you, that motivates your war resistance;

2. Describe an image or moment of resistance, reconcilia-
tion, peacemaking, healing, courage that gives you hope in dark
times.

My desire was to coax the participants into thinking about
why they came, and what motivates their activism. It's been a
hunch of mine for some time that peace activists often come to
be advocates as a result of crystallizing experiences of violence.
As importantly, peace activists have had experiences that give
them hope, that lead them to fight against injustice and oppression, and sharing those moments of hope could be a way to hold
off the darkness.

Once they had done their writing, I prompted them with two
refrains; the first, "For we have seen" would initiate each new
image of violence, and the second, "we work to build a world"
would begin the images of peacemaking and hope. I stood in
the center of the room, searching for and calling on volunteers
ready with their images and words scrawled at the moment.

The instant reading was quite powerful, in ways that the text
below cannot dramatize, a testament to their individual experiences and collective labor. There was an audible crackle in the
silence of the room between each participant's reading, that ex-
change of energy that Muriel Rukeyser proposes is the work of
poetry. Here were a bunch of seasoned peace people, war resisters who were risking even what little they had to refuse money
for wars, who knew the power of action but were not necessar-

ily comfortable with poetry or even their own words; yet each brought their language to bear on the rather mysterious ways in which they had come together for this conference of war tax resistance.

Mindful of that gap (as poetry is almost always what's lost in translation), I share the vestige of that collective symbolic action. I took the pieces that I collected from the participants and built this version, excerpted here:

For we have seen

She struggled hard to live, her eyes closed slowly against the light, and all was dark. What now?

For we have seen

Shots crack the stillness. Sirens scream, a sea of green 70s police units. It's a hideous colon and I don't feel safe. Shooter still at large. Time to walk to school. "You'll be fine," my mother says, and "don't be late."

For we have seen

It was the night of my seventh or eighth birthday, when he locked the front door, pushing me out of his way, to top the window to scream and call my mother a bitch.

For we have seen

Numbers pulled from a jar cleaved a room of young men—a lottery of death that is our job to rescramble.

For we have seen

The heat bore down the blood flowed out of her leg and watered the plants. She who was left there.

For we have seen

Dusty Indian village in evenings cool untouchable side of
   town, sari-clad woman approaches, lifts infant to me and
   says (in translation): "take him to your county and give
   him a good life."

2. We build a world . . .

We build a world

By what right, she the angry one
Do you impugn the sacrifice
Of our brave?
And why don't
You go back to
The country you came from
And the answer that came
I was here before your ancestors.
And my descendants shall carry on
When I am no more.

We build a world

The police officer, tired of her constant crawling through his
   legs, lay fingers in her hair and clenched then into a fist,
   and dragged her screaming across the Pentagon floor,
   twinkling eyes and all.

We build a world

From the knowing fear of dogs and baseball bats on Selma
   bridge to the triumphal march as far as one could see,
   front and back.

We build a world

It was when she was being dragged away and I, I was being
   pushed back, she was on the ground being choked and I
   was being detained when she pulled the cop down with
   her, and kicked him down. We escaped.

We build a world

Awaking to pre-dawn bomb and machinegun fire. It's
   thanksgiving in the U.S.A. No more hiding in Guatemalan
   jungles for 13 years. The call goes out to "illumine all
   the lamps!" and show the U.S.-issue helicopter gunships
   where we are: civilian farmers and human rights witnesses
   standing in the open clearing as targets of strength.

We build a world

A young boy caught a fish and could not get the hook out.
   It was dying, the spiny fins stuck his hands. An older
   boy, a teenager, came along and simply said, "hold the
   fin backwards hard, and pull out the hook," and calmly
   walked away, before the miracle of success.

We build a world

We exchanged war stories. Her ten years from age 12,
   insisting on being allowed a combatant role. Once so
   scared, she turned the gun with its last bullet toward
   herself until the danger passed. "So, how long were you
   there?" "Well," I say, "the usual tour was a year. But I was
   wounded and spent months in the hospital." She stopped
   short and gave a sigh and a look of sorrow. "You were only
   a tourist."

We build a world

Her eyes shining in the lungs of the world looked at us, in
   the Colombian rainforest, and said, I can't believe you
   came all the way here to see me.

Clearly, the language varies from the propagandistic to the
imagistic, and much of it on the page lacks the felt tonalities articulated by the authors of those lines. But the lines themselves
demonstrate the great diversity of experiences that bring together war resisters—from childhood experiences of domestic
violence, to adult encounters of global war, both as soldier and
as activist—as well as the moments of communion and empow-

erment that encourage and sustain peace activists and war resisters. Most importantly, the group became, in the ceremonial
sharing of this poem, a momentary and provisional collectivity—a critical experience for conscientious objectors, whose resistance is often solitary and often sustainable due to the steely
intransigence and hard-fought independence of the objector.
Finally, I would be remiss if I did not also mention how poetry
became alive again, not only for them but also for me, who felt
the dilatory magic of words broken and shared, the meal after
the meal we had eaten together.

Notes

1. Karl Marx, "Comments on James Mill's *Elements of Political Econo-
my*," in *Gesamtausgabe, Erste Abteilung* (Berlin, 1932), quoted in Jon El-
ster, *Karl Marx: A Reader* (New York: Cambridge University Press, 1986),
35.

2. Joseph Beuys, *Joseph Beuys* (Beacon: Dia Art Foundation, 1988),
21.

3. Shara McCallum, *Song of Thieves* (Pittsburgh: University of Pittsburgh Press, 2003), 51.

4. Naomi Shihab Nye, *Red Suitcase: Poems* (Rochester: BOA Editions,
1994), 21.

Dialogue (II)

From "At the Borders
of Our Tongue"

A Dialogue with Fady Joudah

FADY JOUDAH: *Sand Opera* is ultimately a book about love, its
loss and recapture, and the struggle in between. Many will
completely misread it as another book of political poems, in
that reductive, ready-made sense of "political," which is reserved
for certain themes but mostly for certain ethnicities . . . because
it is written by an Arab American.

PHILIP METRES: I love the fact that you read *Sand Opera* as a book
about love. The longer I worked on the book, the more I felt
compelled to move past the dark forces that instigated its
beginnings, forces that threatened to overwhelm it and me.
Love, as much as I can understand it, thrives in an atmosphere
of care for the self and other—the self of the other and the
other of the self—through openness, listening, and dialogue.
Because the book was born in the post-9/11 era, it necessarily
confronts the dark side of oppression, silencing, and torture.
Torture, as Elaine Scarry has explored so powerfully in *The
Body in Pain*, is the diametrical opposite of love, the radical
de-creation of the other for political ends. The recent release
of the so-called "Torture Report" (2014), and the torrent of
responses (both expressions of condemnation and defensive
justifications) have felt like a traumatic repetition for me.
Didn't we deal with this during the Abu Ghraib prison scandal
and the "Enhanced Interrogation" debate? Even now, the
political conversation seems to skip over the fact that torture
contravenes international law and is a profoundly immoral act,
and moves so quickly to debate its merits—whether any good
"intelligence" may have been gleaned from it. Why is it that the

writers who have gained the widest platforms were veterans of the war, some of whom participated directly in interrogation—for example, Eric Fair's courageous 2014 Letter to the Editor in *The New York Times*—while Arab voices, like Iraqi writer Sinan Antoon's, are so hard to find and so marginalized?

FJ: Yes, *Good Morning Vietnam, Platoon, Apocalypse Now*, and now it's *American Sniper*. The question of agency is a serious one here. It's what I call the Oliver Stone Syndrome, where the humanity of the victimized is further diluted by the humanity of the victimizer who just can't let go of their moral agony. Or in Edward Said's words, it is "the permission to narrate."[1] Agency belongs to those who have tortured or shot Arabs and lived to tell about it. It is literature's version of the Patriot Act, behind the mask of "professionalism," "plurality," and "experience." The representatives of power's soft remorseful side get the front row tickets at the table of public discourse.

PM: The recent events reminded me how dismayed I was by American representations of Abu Ghraib. Take Errol Morris' documentary "Standard Operating Procedure." Here was this careful examination of how the prison scandal unfolded, through the eyes of the perpetrators, and NOT ONE of the victims was interviewed. Their presence was merely fodder for the exercise of imperial remorse. And it seems to be happening again.

I should make it clear, at the same time, the important work of American veterans speaking out about against acts of abuse or atrocity and owning complicity with larger structures of oppression. As I've learned personally from my father, a Vietnam veteran and Arab American, American veterans carry a particular burden of grief and guilt that makes it complicated for them to speak publicly. We may have already reached the moment where veteran casualties from suicide now have passed combat fatalities. So the war continues for our veterans, something I broach in *Sand Opera* in "The Blues of Ken Davis," "The Blues of Joe Darby," "War Stories," "Home Sweet Home," and "Breathing Together." Brian Turner, Hugh Martin, and Roy Scranton are crucial voices in the conversation. But we have to face the fact that American culture is addicted to the war story.

My hope is that the veteran writers recognize the platform that our militarized culture grants them and pull on that stage, as it were, the Arab and Muslim voices that would be treated with skepticism or unheard entirely. In "Meet the Poet-Stranger," Khaled Mattawa shares a painful anecdote about a reading that he and Dunya Mikhail, an Iraqi poet, did with Brian Turner, at which every single question during the "Q" & "A" afterward was addressed to Brian. That could have been a moment to move the conversation in a new direction.

FJ: In what ways, then, does *Sand Opera* address the navel-gazing guilt in America over the horror it committed against Iraqis? I mean most of what we read about Iraq, or I should say most American literature that is pushed to the front about Iraq, is about our national imperial humanity. Iraqis remain dead people to pity, ghosts for our Ouija board, and when they have voices, it is actually a reflection of how morally virtuous our voices are (as poets, journalists, or novelists). It seems even when they speak, they speak through us. We are the ventriloquists of the dead we kill.

PM: You're asking a difficult question, one that readers of *Sand Opera* may have to answer for themselves. That question of representation has haunted me as well, maybe because I've learned about Iraq partly through the frame of the anti-war movement, which often hyperfocuses on Iraqi victimization. Do we still have to go back to Edward Said's notion of Orientalism—the fact that American perceptions of the Middle East are saturated by imperial thinking? We have to get past our *Heart of Darkness* obsession and move into *Things Fall Apart*, and past that.

When I think about my history with Iraq—this country that I've never visited but that has visited me in the eyes and lives of Iraqi people I've met and befriended, alongside the roil and static of representations of Iraq—I go back to 1990, during the Iraq invasion of Kuwait, the advent of U.S.-led economic sanctions, and the subsequent Persian Gulf War of 1991. I organized a rally against the war on my college campus, the first anti-war demonstration at Holy Cross College probably since the Vietnam War. Just a couple months later, I watched my classmates watching George Bush the First announce that bombing had begun, and the excitement was palpable. The coverage by U.S. media, dogged by conservative accusations that they had lost the Vietnam War, was surreal. It utterly lacked journalistic integrity, and good people lost their critical distance in the patriotic buzz of "smart" bombs and the myth of surgical strikes and a "clean" war. I felt as if someone had stolen my country, that the culture had gone psychotic. The Amiriyah shelter massacre, in which a U.S. "smart" bomb killed four hundred civilians in a bomb shelter during the bombing of Iraq, barely made the news.

When the truth of the devastation wrought by those bombings emerged, we learned that U.S. forces targeted civilian infrastructure such as water filtration facilities and the electrical grid, and that we had bombed Iraq into a kind of quasi-Stone Age. According to some U.N. humanitarian reports, the consequences of bombing and sanctions led to the deaths of hundreds of thousands of people, often by preventable disease, due to lack of sanitary water and medicine.

There is this horror. In 1996, on "60 Minutes," Leslie Stahl asked U.S. Secretary of State Madeline Albright whether the death of half a million Iraqi children [from sanctions in Iraq] was a price worth paying. Albright replied: "This is a very hard choice . . . but we think the price is worth it."[2] During graduate school at Indiana University, I was a leader in the anti-sanctions campaign, working with peace activists and local Iraqis in Bloomington. We did a number of actions, including raising funds and sending basic medical supplies to Iraq despite the sanctions.

So when I think of Iraq, I think first of Shakir Mustafa and Nawal Nasrallah, two dear friends whom I met in the English Department at Indiana. Shakir was completing his Ph.D. in Irish Literature and Nawal was working in Bloomington and preparing (literally and figuratively) for her wonderful Iraqi cookbook, *Delights from the Garden of Eden*. When I think of Iraq, I think of the wistfulness of their eyes, the melancholy of exile, the graciousness of their hospitality. That's partly why I wrote "A Toast," as a gratitude to the meals that Nawal prepared for us, to honor how they carried their country in exile kitchens.

When I think of Iraq, I think of the Iraqi professor Saleh Altoma at Indiana University, who translated Iraqi poets and shared their poems as part of our local anti-sanctions campaign. I think of his wit and passion, how his mouth would come to a froth as he translated the words of poets into the language of empire, the empire squeezing the throat of his country.

When I think of Iraq, I think of Kadhim Shaaban, an older gentleman who always wore a suit and tie. He would take periodic trips back to Iraq with medical supplies and come back laden with stories of the material and psychological devastation he witnessed. One of his stories inspired my poem "one more story" in *To See the Earth*, which describes his chance meeting with a hungry and scared Iraqi refugee wandering the streets of Amsterdam, looking for her husband, having illegally crossed many borders stowed in a fruit truck.

When I think of Iraq, I think of the scholar who wrote to me from Baghdad, asking for any recent articles about the poetry of Elizabeth Bishop. I think of Nuha al-Radi and her *Baghdad Diaries* and Salam Abdulmunem (a.k.a. "Salam Pax") and his blog missives illuminating life in Iraq from 2003. I think of the Iraqi poets and writers translated into (or writing in) English: Dunya Mikhail, Sinan Antoon, Saadi Youssef, Fadhil al-Azzawi, Amal al-Jubouri, and the fantastic recent anthology, *We Are Iraqis*. And everyone should read Wafaa Bilal's *Shoot an Iraqi*, which will break your heart, and Manal Omar's *Barefoot in Baghdad*.

They are Iraq to me. They are the Iraq I carry.

There are, of course, other Iraqs, many Iraqs, and one shouldn't have to say that, except for the fact that Orientalism constantly flattens all of these Iraqs into "something sinister" (to quote Hayan Charara's poem).[3]

I haven't even begun talking about the recent Iraq War. *Sand Opera* began out of a desire to write back against the dehumanizing force of the Abu Ghraib prison scandal, but I realized very quickly that writing about the photos would simply reinstantiate the position of Iraqi as objectivized victim, a representation ultimately no more human than the Iraqi as a Saddam-following scimitar-wielding maniac. When I found transcripts of the testimonies of the Iraqis who were abused in Abu Ghraib, I knew I wanted to work with them, to work myself into listening to those voices—voices of great vulnerability, but voices that announce their courageous tenacity and will to live. And that, of course, was only the beginning. I wanted to avoid staying in that prison, the prison of Abu Ghraib and the prison of misprision, of seeing Iraqis as victims only.

FJ: You also address the architecture of violence in your book. Those schematic drawings of torture rooms, for example. The book comes close to embodying the physicality of horror, while the juxtaposing text is so tender and humanizing, and is in the voice of the detained, not the victimizer's self-absorbed reflective gaze.

PM: In the process of reading and trying to make sense of how the War on Terror was being conducted abroad, I began to be aware of the use of secret prisons for interrogation, what are called "black sites." (A gruesome and inaccurate depiction of this can be found in the depressingly fawning *Zero Dark Thirty*). One particular article in *Salon* about the story of Yemeni citizen Mohamed Farag Ahmad Bashmilah struck me with force, partly because it included renderings of drawings that Bashmilah had made while in various black sites around the world—probably in order to make sense of where he was and what was happening to him. I wanted to include Bashmilah's version of those spaces, in all their painstaking detail (right down to the broken-down Russian-made jeep outside one compound). His testimony, taken from the legal case against Jeppesen Dataplan for its complicity in shuttling secret prisoners for the CIA, is full of such stunning detail—about the scar on the doctor who examined him, the Rubik's Cube he was given, the plastic water bottles that revealed what country he was in, the sounds of voices beyond the compound wall—that I wanted his longing to appear in some proximity to the solid walls of imprisonment.

The Alice James folks proposed the use of some vellum paper overlays for parts of the book, and we agreed that the language from the testimony should appear as vellum overlays on the black site drawings, which are spread out in the book. The rest of his testimony appears at the end of the book, in a sequence called "Homefront/The Removes," juxtaposed against my own Arab American experiences of 9/11.

FJ: Also there is so much emphasis on music here; the title has Opera in it, the opening sequence is an Aria. It reminds me of a line from an early Darwish poem: "The music of human flesh."[4] Is *Sand Opera* in part also about the cultural construct of art, which is surely a political process one-step removed? In other words, *Sand Opera* denies the exclusion of one form of gaze from another (away or toward politics) and merges both into one. Its truth-seeking does not conveniently sieve art from the politics of its creation.

PM: The title itself is an erasure of the longer (secret) title, revealed on the title page, Standard Operating Procedure. In the early 2000s, WikiLeaks sent me the Standard Operating Procedure manual for the Guantanamo Bay prison. After hesitating for a moment, wondering whether I should open this file at all, I decided that I had an obligation to read further. What I discovered was a dry document of protocols for running a detention facility; but in some of its details, it demonstrated a remarkable amount of cultural sensitivity—about how to handle a Qu'ran properly, and more ominously, how to conduct a proper Muslim burial. The fact that this was the place where Qu'rans would be thrown in the toilet and men forcibly smeared in the face with menstrual blood suggests the gulf between U.S. law (and cultural knowledge) and the conduct of military intelligence and CIA in the War on Terror.

As Walter Benjamin once said, every artifact of civilization is also an artifact of barbarism.[5] I wanted to mention this first because as I wrote the poems that would comprise *Sand Opera*, I did not want to succumb to the temptation of aestheticizing the violence, of making the horrors beautiful. The notion that suffering can be redemptive, or that "beauty can save the world" (*pace* Dostoyevsky)[6] seem to me to be dubious and even dangerous. Yet at the same time, there is no life without suffering, and what would life be without beauty? In writing a book that tried to work with life as I've known it during the War on Terror, I could not but enter into the caves of human pain— my own and others'. At the same time, I wanted to write a book that would testify to the persistence and beauty of our tenacity not only to survive but to live with verve and delve into delight. Personally, the War on Terror has overlapped precisely with my life as a father to two beautiful girls. Everything about this book is asking the question that my daughter asked to me, when we heard over the radio an Iraqi man keen: "is that man crying or singing?"

Sand Opera employs the tropes of opera in its structure and themes. The book's sections, as in classic opera, reference both "arias" and "recitatives," the two dominant modes of opera, roughly corresponding to lyric and narrative/dramatic modes in poetry. The book isn't meant to be a libretto, though I imagine it could be staged as a play. The "abu ghraib arias," for example, are composed of both blues poems written from the point of view of American military personally and arias written from the point of view of Iraqi detainees, and together these could be seen as a mini-opera.

FJ: And yet you take this further. *Sand Opera* is also a mosaic of poetic forms. The intensity of the music does not let up. It's as if I have to second-guess my lungs, when to inhale and when to exhale.

PM: The longer I write poetry, the more interested I've become in poetic practice as a kind of trance state—or three interlinked trance states of writing, reading, and reciting. We think of the origins of poetry as multiple: its dialogue with the tribe (in the form we come to know as the epic), its dialogue with the gods or others (lyric), and its dialogue with action (drama). Is it any surprise that the dialogue with otherness that is the lyric is named for its relationship to the ancient stringed instrument, the lyre? What is music but organized noise, some incantatory relationship between repetition and variation? The first poetry was most likely incantatory, ecstatic, otherworldly—from Sumerian prayers to Sappho's lyrics, from the Psalms to the shamanic spells transcribed in *Technicians of the Sacred.*

Sand Opera is rife with poems that employ recursion and even rhyme—some of them in fairly traditional poetic forms such as the sonnet ("Etruscan Cista Handle"), the pantoum ("Testimony"), heroic couplets ("*When I Was a Child, I Lived as a Child,* I Said to My Dad"), and the sestina ("The Iraqi Curator's PowerPoint"). And it begins and ends with poem-prayers ("Illumination of the Martyrdom of St. Sebastian" and "Compline") that aspire to a poetry of trance, opening a door to the spirit world, where we can consult with ancestors who might bring balm to our wounds. In the Catholic tradition, prior to eating God's body, entering into communion with the Eternal, the believer says: "O Lord, I am not worthy that you should enter under my roof, but only say the word and my soul shall be healed."

FJ: As you mentioned, your daughters make beautiful appearances in *Sand Opera.* It is perhaps the most touching and exalting part of the book, for me, at least, as a father.

PM: This is where we circle back to the centrality of love. "Hung Lyres," the sequence of autobiographical lyric poems, meditate on what it means to be a parent in an age of terror. I think of the vulnerability and tenderness of my daughters' infant bodies—their pliable and open ears, their sweet noses, their gooey mouths, their alien and familiar eyes. I don't think my wife and I slept for five years, as they cried themselves awake and asleep in their young babyhoods. We were constantly sleep-deprived and nerve-shot, and yet all we knew to do was to keep on doing what we must do—to nurture, to calm, to feed, to change, to bathe, to press our flesh to flesh.

I remember when Adele was born; I was in awe of the beauty of her ears. Her ears, of all things! I guess I couldn't have imagined that she had ears, curled up in her mother's womb. And that these beautiful doors to the world could never be shut except by one's hands. That our bodies are that open, that exposed.

To think that at the same time, people were being tortured by use of constant, ear-splitting sound in Guantanamo Bay prison. Such unrelenting noise, with the most ludicrous of soundtracks—the Barney Theme Song, for example: *I love you, you love me, we're a happy family, with a great big hug and a kiss from me to you, won't you say you love me too.* I can't imagine a more sinister song to play to someone constantly day and night. That shit would drive anyone crazy.

"Hung Lyres" is about the simultaneity of these two realities, and ends with something amazing that my daughter once said on a walk after a rainy day outside, when all the worms have been flung or flung themselves onto the sidewalk. One of my favorite poems of yours, "Mimesis," is so simple and so wise, something your daughter said to you. Sometimes poetry is listening, listening to the great listeners.

Just last night, I dreamt that I got separated from my wife and daughter at the airport and ended up in Gaza, alone, and Israeli security was hounding me, accusing me of being a terrorist, trying to force me into a plane back to the United States. I was trying to explain to the interrogator that I wasn't alone, that my wife and daughter would be here soon, but she pushed me into a holding pen—neither in Palestine nor in America. Later, I was walking beneath a large salty dune, and the dune collapsed, covering me completely in sand.

When I woke, I remembered where I was. How easy it is to get drowned in oppression, how easy to get cut off from the resources of our love.

FJ: Allow me to return to what you said about our American addiction to the war story. How we don't recognize that we as a nation have been in perpetual war. So much of what empire touches turns to stone, medusa becomes our lot. Yet what is most celebrated in American letters, its "pop" presence, with all its puns, stifles a meaningful sense of resistance. What is most permissible, most "us," is what sings our eternal eulogy. Everything else is under the surveillance of "criticism." It's as if a bizarre phobia of national death overtakes our vision of what art can do. The art turns tribal, but the tribe is massive. The "I" is set down already scripted paths, even for those who argue against the "I." The paths may be numerous, but they have been well trodden: algorithmic bifurcations and diagrams.

110

PM: Perhaps that fear's origins may be deeply unconscious. Perhaps Americans have a dim awareness that we may be partly responsible for or complicit in the deep inequities, not only in our own society but also between our society and those of the rest of the world. And that, if fate were different and I were on the other side of that inequity, I might too come to resent and resist this massive, tentacular, flexible, omnipresent yet nebulous network of power we know as empire. So that fear, that impulse for security, is not necessarily merely some national limbic system reaction or survival instinct, but rather an expression of our own awareness of our complicity with injustice. Poetry cannot heal these wounds alone; but it's my primary technology of diagnosis and therapeutic practice.

I am grateful, Fady, to have met you a decade ago through Radius of Arab American Writers, when I submitted poems for the RAWI website. Your editorial advice was impassioned and surgical, and I immediately felt that I was in the presence of a brother in the work of poetry. And more than that: I've found our conversations to be deeply inspiring, challenging me to explore my own wounds and blind spots. One thing that we've done as a community of Arab American writers for each other is to confirm that we're not alone, and that we're not crazy. That the society in which we live may occasionally "deny us the grace of rage," as you said once, quoting another postcolonial writer, Arundhati Roy,[7] but that it won't silence us or cause us to reduce our complex, irreducible humanity. To believe that we are boxed in by politics is an illusion, though it's also true that we find ourselves in the dynamics of "minor literature."[8] There isn't a theme or a form or a possibility in poetry that should be kept from us. We both have been experimenting with love poetry, and it's not an allegory for the Middle East!

FJ: And "love poetry" may also be a direct expression for the desire to love, simple as that. The poet Tanya Foster recently reminded me of the Umbra poets of the early 1960s, who were cognizant their imposed singularities did not add up to a collective presence. Whenever one of them was invited to a reading, he or she brought others from the group along and read together. In other words, those Black poets were decontextualized from the relation they held within their community and from the relation America at large had with them. So those poets resisted the island existence, so to speak. They were singular plurals, and they stood up to make it known. Do you see this repeat itself today regarding Arab and Muslim American poets, for example?

PM: Let's do it that way. The Umbra poets laid the groundwork for the Black Arts Movement just a few years later, which had a profound impact on American poetry. They forced American poetry to confront its aesthetics and politics of whiteness in ways that still reverberate; every time a new anthology of American poetry emerges, the dialogues within African American poetry (our most American of American poetry, to my mind) emerge again—about the place of politics, audience, and the telos of art. There is now a space and tradition for radical American poetry, and this is one of its primary sources.

It's been beautiful to see the reception of Claudia Rankine's important book, *Citizen*. It appears, at last, we are having a conversation about the insidious psychological damage of racism. I love that the book explores not only various personal punctures of racism (what is modern racism but death by a thousand cuts?) but also the very public meltdowns of Serena Williams and the Algerian soccer star Zinedine Zidane—due to racial attacks. I was shocked when reading *Citizen* how I kept nodding my head and seeing connections between it and various poems in your recent book *Textu* (both in terms of content and form, like a sort of Morse code of the margins slipping into the cells of texts) and *Sand Opera*, particularly the "Homefront/Removes" sequence, about what it was like post-9/11 for Arabs and Muslims in America. Is America ready to have this conversation? I really hope so.

But back to the big question. I don't know whether our impact will be similar to Umbra or the Black Arts Movement. But here's a modest forecast. I believe we are in the opening phase of an Arab American literary renaissance, an "al-Mahjar" 2.0, hearkening back to the early twentieth century flourishing of Arab American letters known as the Pen Group: Ameen Rihani, Kahlil Gibran, and Michael Naimy. The first throes of a revolution. Our elders are Lawrence Joseph and Naomi Shihab Nye and Mahmoud Darwish and Etel Adnan and Adonis and Ammiel Alcalay. I hereby nominate Naomi Shihab Nye as the next U.S. poet laureate. Can you imagine someone more prepared to spread the Gospel of Poetry as a medium of joy, an articulation of our joie de vivre?

FJ: But to be a U.S. poet laureate, you have to disavow the political; you cannot talk about any issues that trouble imperial politics.

Citizen is about microaggression, and yes, I liked it deeply. But do you think an equally well-envisioned book about Ferguson, for example, would reach the same heights in American culture? There's a safety in *Citizen* with which it enters and exits the lungs of the grand American narrative, the permissible. I think *Citizen*'s genius is its limitation, its capacity to show us that the permissible in American letters includes, for the most part, bourgeois enactments or representation of racism. Traditionally, it has been that when solid middle-class sensibility is moved in America (thus all the fascination with *Citizen*'s use of the second-person pronoun) that a morality or the illusion of morality begins to shift inside America. This undressing is what I admire about *Citizen*. The crowd is clapping because it is finally looking in the mirror and sighing at what it sees. As if Godot has finally arrived. It always amazed me how steeped in politics American letters are, yet they remain in "projective identification" about it. It is often the "other" non-citizen citizen or non-American American whose art is "political."

You also mentioned "postcolonial" twice so far. How are Arabs and Muslims postcolonial subjects of American empire? If anything, many are being recolonized. What is American culture's track record in managing its postcolonial or colonial (or vanquished) subjects? Is an Iraqi closer to a Vietnamese? Isn't there something vulgar about a hierarchy of belonging (within empire) through a classification of suffering the empire? The inevitability of what we write, so far as it reaffirms, even if unintentionally, the narrative of our American goodness which, in part, includes in its folds their origin's shortcomings, their stereotypes.

PM: Fady, as usual you've homed in on the essence of the problem, one that will not be resolved by our conversation. As poets, we bridle against the false freedoms and protected zones of the Literary. Publication is the auction of the mind, as Dickinson once wrote. Each poem becomes a labor against those preapproved pathways. The institutions of the Literary are no more liberated than any other institution, subject to internal and external rules. In the end, what binds us as poets is our concern for language and its possibilities. The perceived leftism of poetry—related to its position in the post-1960s university culture—is bounded and rhetorical, to be sure. Every gesture of radicalism, in our absorptive system, seems so quickly domesticated and commodified. So we're damned by our success or damned by the haters. I try not to worry too much about reception. We know that there will be haters and dismissers. But let awake people be awake.

In terms of the wider literary question, I come back to the inherent scholarly tension between canonicity and literary history. If canonicity is often the mechanism of hierarchy and exclusion, then literary history may be the mechanism of dilation and inclusion; in this struggle, I hope that I'm part of the operation of inclusion. That's deeply connected to the question of the postcolonial, moving through the questions in the work of Edward Said and Gayatri Spivak.

Okay, this has compelled me to name some names. Our brother Khaled Mattawa, who brought me into the RAWI community, recently received the MacArthur Genius Grant for his poetry and his voluminous translations from the Arab world. You won the Yale Younger Poetry prize and the Griffin Prize for your translations of Ghassan Zaqtan. There's Hayan Charara with three gut-punching books of poems and the important anthology *Inclined to Speak*, Suheir Hammad, Farid Matuk, Deema Shehabi, Nathalie Handal, Glenn Shaheen, Samiya Bashir, Matthew Shenoda, Siwar Masannat, Hala Alyan, Zeina Hashem Beck, Mohja Kahf, Elmaz Abinader, Hedy Habra, Lisa Suhair Majaj, Carolina Ebeid, Angele Ellis, Ahimsa Timoteo Bodhran, Rewa Zeinati, Priscilla Wathington, Remi Kanazi, Eliot Khalil Wilson, George Abraham, Tariq Luthun, Jess Rizkallah, Peter Twal, Nuar Alsadir, Marwa Helal. Our work is as aesthetically varied as we are. Every time I turn around, another Arab American or Arab Anglophone poet has a new book of poems. I've not even mentioned the phenomenal poets from the Muslim world: Kazim Ali, Shadab Hashmi, Safia Elhillo, Persis Karim, Ladan Osman, Zohra Saed, Solmaz Sharif, Kaveh Akbar. Marilyn Hacker should be mentioned for her translations of and support for Arab poets. I think of the American poets and writers who stand with us, as we stand with them, trying to breathe and speak together.

To answer your question: we, too, sing America, in our own way.

Americans will hear not (only) themselves in us, but how they are not themselves alone, and that none of us can continue to live as if our definition of humanity ends at our national borders, at the borders of our skin, or at the borders of our tongue.

1. Edward Said, "Permission to Narrate," *London Review of Books* 6.3 (1984): 13–17.

2. *60 Minutes*, "Punishing Saddam," CBS News, May 12, 1996.

3. Hayan Charara, *Something Sinister* (Pittsburgh: Carnegie Mellon Press, 2016).

4. Mahmoud Darwish, "The Wandering Guitar Player," in *The Music of Human Flesh*, trans. Denys Johnson Davies (Portsmouth: Heinemann, 1980), 55.

5. Walter Benjamin, "Theses on the Philosophy of History," in *Illuminations* (New York: Harcourt, 1940).

6. Fyodor Dostoevsky, *The Idiot*, trans. Constance Garnett (Portsmouth: Heinemann, 1913).

7. Arundhati Roy, "The Greater Common Good," *End of Imagination* (Chicago: Haymarket Books, 1998), 148.

8. Gilles Deleuze and Felix Guattari, "What Is a Minor Literature?" in *Kafka: Toward a Minor Literature* (Minneapolis: University of Minnesota Press, 1986).

Essays & Portraits (II)

Lang/scapes

War Resistance Poetry in Public Spaces

> Citizens behave as a public body when they confer in
> an unrestricted fashion—that is, with the guarantee of
> freedom of assembly and association and the freedom to
> express and publish their opinions—about matters of gen-
> eral interest. In a large public body this kind of commu-
> nication requires specific means for transmitting informa-
> tion and influencing those who receive it. . . . We speak of
> the public sphere in contrast, for instance, to the literary
> one, when public discussion deals with objects connected
> to the activity of the state.
> —Jurgen Habermas[1]

> Freedom of the Press is limited to those who own one.
> —A. J. Liebling[2]

Liebling's sarcastic take on freedom of the press, in stark contrast to Habermas' idealized theorization of the public sphere,
lays bare a fundamental tension in the construction of a nation's
self-narrations. Who gets to speak, and whose voice is heard in
our national conversations about the direction of our country?
The abyss between the words "representative" and "democracy" that define our form of government extends even wider in
our times when so many people bitterly opposed the Iraq war
that the few—the few who claim authorship of our national
narrative—were unwilling to end. In an age when there appears
to be an almost infinite number of digital platforms to let one's
voice "be heard," some voices are heard, to echo Orwell, more
loudly than others.

119

Poetry has refused to roll over and keep dreaming. It has bolted upright, and gotten out of bed—that is, off the page—and into other spaces where people don't usually expect to find it. In the conclusion to *Behind the Lines*, I made a post-Gutenbergian call to see poetry breathe outside of the confines of books, and for us to see poetry freed into the third dimension of public spaces: "war resistance poems thus ask for our redeployment in multiple sites, returning poetry to where it thrives—at the local and in local resistance [i.e., "behind the lines" and beyond the page and into the public square]—as graffiti, in pamphlets, as performances, as songs, and in the classroom."[3] This poetry invites us "to find ways of making poetry 'active' again, and making activism a labor of making as much as a labor of protest and unmasking."[4] Though books can be liberatory sites for poetry—as they have been for so many readers of poetry over the centuries—the culture of poetry remained mostly a culture of the book, to the detriment of poetry's vital relationship to orality, to performance, to embodiment.

During our imperial age, I continue to find signs that war resistance poetry is hardly moribund and often lives in the form of signs themselves: hijacked billboards, scrawled bedsheets, homemade placards, spray-painted bullets of compressed language suddenly visible in landscapes usually denuded of poetic speech-acts. I propose to call this poetry *lang/scape*, words sutured into landscapes (both literal and figurative). The word "landscape," after all, comes from the Dutch root "*schap*," which likely comes from "*skap*," meaning "to create, ordain, appoint." Related to the Anglian "*scip*," which means "a state, condition of being," these *lang/scapes* are made words that attempt to bring a vision of resistance into being. On faculty office doors, in secluded parks, at peace shows, in poetry readings in reading halls and on the streets, later YouTubed for the Internet masses, above freeway overpasses, on roadside fences—war resistance poetry has laid claim to spaces typically reserved for advertisements and safety signs, sutured the space between the public sphere and the literary sphere, and created its own presses and transient pages to voice the growing weariness and outrage at the Iraq War—a war initiated through falsified evidence, conducted with arrogant short-sightedness, and criminally mismanaged.

120

To call such language acts *poems* is to interrogate not only page-based definitions of poetry but also definitions of poetry that privilege difficulty, complexity, and ambiguity above all else. Such poetry—with its limited and fugitive palettes—cannot manifest the "difficulty" made possible by a larger field; yet, the examples of *lang/scape* that most fully deserve to be called "poetry" provoke in multiple ways—not merely as agitprop, whose messages are always and necessarily transparent—and induce further rumination by their audiences. As a page-centered, occasionally difficult poet, and a reader of poetry who finds pleasure in the page and in complexity, I worry that my claim veers close to the argument that all political speech (for example, former Secretary of Defense Donald Rumsfeld's dodgy discourse at press conferences) is necessarily a kind of poetry.

Yet poetry is never merely an extension of political rhetoric. On the contrary, as Susan Schultz has written, "Rumsfeld wants to get people off his scent so he can do things. [Poetry] is the scent, you could say—it's really trying to get you deep into a cultural moment or political moment, or just into how language works."[5] *Lang/scape*, then, worries that line between the poetic and the political. When it succeeds, it enables political thinking without being reducible to sloganeering. It allows us to see rhetorical language for what it is—rhetorical language—not for what it promises (that it contains the whole truth). It provides both dissenters and the wider citizenry insight into the possibilities and limits of symbolic action itself as a kind of language—one of the critical modes of nonviolent protest. Finally, it compels us to imagine new landscapes, as it were, within the landscape itself.

While these signs of life speak to poetry's vital intervention as a mode of dissent, they also admit to their (occasionally extreme) marginality by virtue of their transience, their unrepeatability, their limited discursive space, even their questionable legality. Yet these quixotic and sometimes beautiful acts coax and cajole us, their readers, not simply to talk back, but to commensurate action—they are flashes of light that illuminate a way in the thicket of our despair.

The following examples of *lang/scape* begin with the local, since *lang/scape* arguably attempts to reclaim the local as a site of independent speech and thought. Then I turn to more far-flung national examples. *Lang/scape* offers a vital example of how the local and the global intertwine and converse with one another; *lang/scape*, like dissent itself, attains double-resonance as a result of its information-dissemination networks of the Internet. Neither merely local, nor just global, such poetry makes claims to suture these disparate audiences and to participate in larger conversations about the future narrations of the nation (and of the globe).

B(e)aring Witness: Demonstrations

When Habermas speaks of the "public body," his language refers back to the archeology of political language; from the notion of the King as the physical manifestation of God and State to the more recent formulations of anxiety over "illegal aliens" penetrating the borders of the national body, politics so frequently measures the relationships of bodies to the other bodies. Whether one ascribes to the Habermasian ideal of bodies "confer[ring] in an unrestricted fashion"[6] or the Foucauldian notion of society revolving around the disciplining of bodies, what bodies are allowed to do is an intricate matter of politics. If, as von Clausewitz proposed, war is the pursuit of politics by other means, then war resistance in times of limited free speech may sometimes require its own political actions, outside of the normal channels of information dissemination.

On November 12, 2002, Donna Oehm Sheehan and a cohort of friends who were disturbed by the drumbeats to war literalized Habermas' bodies "behav[ing] as a public body . . . confer[ring] in an unrestricted fashion"[7] when they decided to strip their clothes and form the word that they wished would come into being: *peace*. Sheehan, founder of "Baring Witness," a group demonstrating against the then-impending Iraq War recalled a dream that she had

> of people creating artistic shapes with their bodies. My thoughts went to Helen Odeworitse and 600 Nigerian women, who used the threat of their nakedness (a shaming gesture for

men in Nigeria and perhaps elsewhere?) to force Chevron-Texaco to listen to their families' needs. The women's action of occupying the oil terminal and threatening to shame the male employees made Chevron concede to their demands to share a little of the wealth by providing basic services to the local people.

That was such a powerful image for me at the time that it became a natural extension of my thoughts about my dream. Now I saw women's bodies forming letters—and the word they formed had to be PEACE.

From that inspired moment, I turned to the resource that all organizers need—their like-minded friends. "Do you think we could do it?" Yes, yes, and yes! We came up with the perfect photographer who decided the perfect, accessible location with grass, a horizon and parking. We called the owners for permission to use the field on Tuesday afternoon. . . . The excitement and nervousness grew as the vision became a possibility. The huge question was whether women would be able to withstand the vulnerability of exposing themselves nude. Each of us called five women and told them to call five more apiece. Many women responded with the same excitement and willingness, some could not attend. The few who could make it and were excited by the idea but were unwilling to disrobe were invited to help with the clothes. By Tuesday, over 50 women turned up at the field.[8]

Baring Witness' bodily performance of "peace" is a kind of language—not only on the level of content, of course, but also on the level of form. The very bodies which are exposed—exposed, of course, not only to the elements but to the documentary and predatory camera's eye—speak back to the casual viewer with a stark conviction, a conviction beyond shame. When I first read about this act, my reflex response was narrowly judgmental: "the hippies of Marin County have made the peace movement yet again look self-serving and out of step with the rest of the country." The image-hungry mass media rapidly consumed the story, crashing Baring Witness' web servers. Yet in Paul Reffel's reflection on the media coverage, "Baring Witness: The New Peace Movement," he notes the awkwardness with which two male broadcasters handled this image:

When the image of the PEACE photo was shown on CBS Sunday Morning as a segue between "news" items, Charles Osgood's voice-over was a respectful statement of the facts, but when he came on camera, he said, "Talk about a body of work." Then he turned to introduce Bob Schieffer, who said, "I was hoping for a close-up." Many women were offended by these typical male responses, but what do they really convey? These are the kind of stock responses that men express when they get together. They form a mask of bravado, which is a survival tactic for men among men. What they really show is the embarrassment most sober men feel when confronted by public female nudity. Bob Schieffer's body language—grinning, his eyes down and head slightly bowed—revealed not leering priapism but self-conscious uncertainty, even as he spoke the words that he was "expected" to say. That is part of the dilemma of appearing "manly" in America.[9]

In the years that followed, similar demonstrations—by women and men—spread throughout the world. Though, clearly, the contexts in which American women and men deploy their nakedness as a sign of vulnerability may differ from the Nigerian social context (in which the threat of stripping had been enough to change policy), the "baring witness" nonetheless remains a powerful, if contradictory, witness.

Demonstrations (2): How Does the Peace Movement Represent Itself?

On Labor Day 2007, some poetry students and I met in downtown Cleveland's Willard Park to engage in a project called "Stories of War and Peace," gathering oral narratives from people working at or attending The Peace Show. A Cleveland event since 2002, the Peace Show began as a response to the Air Show, which members of the Catholic Worker and other radical pacifist groups had been picketing as a celebration of militarism. The idea of the Peace Show was to move beyond the negativism of protest to a "pro-attestation" (Allen Ginsberg's coinage)—i.e., a celebration of what we believe and how we live out the sentence of those beliefs. The students and I gathered over fifty interviews in a few hours, met and talked with many more than that—from groups whose issues spanned the progressive gamut from veganism to peace in the Middle East.

Jonathan LaGuardia, a graduate student at John Carroll University, reflected on the experience of listening:

Early in the day, I tagged along on an interview with a Vietnam Veteran, a clean-shaven man of about 60, dressed in a Vietnam-era army shirt and a pair of dull gray cotton shorts. He carried an American flag on a pole over his shoulder in which the separate little white stars—one for each country in the Union—was replaced by a peace sign.

When we started the recorder and asked him to introduce himself, he began factually—basic training at such and such a location, elevated in rank to such and such a position, eventually stationed just north of Saigon—though it quickly turned to personal loss: "Two days after [the January 31, 1968 offensive]," he said, "one of my lieutenants was killed. It was a huge shock to me, and it's still"—his voice began to break, and his eyes shifted from the tiny microphone he had been watching to some remote, unidentifiable position in the distance— "and, ummm, it's going to be a shock to me for the rest of my life."

A little while into the interview, after more factual "I was here and then went there," the subject of death came up again, and again the speaker hesitated, staring off into the distance and letting his lip quiver before regaining control. His hesitations were so perfect that I could not help but view them as performances—staged, rehearsed performances of the same talk he had been giving for the last 40 years.

About four or five hours later, an Iraq Vet came up to me, a black man about my age with short, loose dreadlocks and no visible wounds. He came up to me not to give a story, but to give his name and contact information, in case we'd like to get in touch with him at some point in the future. "I'm sure you'll want to hear what I have to say," he said, "but my head just isn't straight enough to submit to an interview yet."

So, here I have these two generations of veterans: the Vietnam Veteran whose grief seemed rehearsed, and the Iraq Veteran who, in his own words, couldn't get his head "straight enough" to submit to an interview. When the Iraq Vet left me, I turned to where we had interviewed the Vietnam Vet, and there he was still, parading up and down the grass with his American Peace Flag over his shoulder—this 60 year old man in a long sleeved army shirt in the sweltering sun had been walking back and forth for 4 solid hours for no other reason than to be there, to be seen.

With this sight, I saw new value to his performance, thinking that there was a truth to the performed grief that immediate grief could not have delivered. Perhaps it took those 40 years to put those moments into a coherent narrative, the truth of his performed grief identical to his somber but dedicated march: exhausting, but necessary.[10]

LaGuardia's meditation offers us the fundamental problem at the heart of so much war poetry; the way we approach language to articulate our experience—whether it is hardened into a rote speech or still beyond our words—does not ensure successful communication of information. Rather, almost by necessity, the putting-into-language of traumatic experience—whether oral narrative, written story, or poetry—becomes itself a kind of new experience that the listener completes.

Finally, one of the many entertainments at the Peace Show— in addition to information booths, children's activities such as face-painting, food and drink, stilt-walkers, and a paper Peace Plane "launch"—was a main stage of music, rap, and poetry. Competing with the ear-splitting sound of Air Show military jets frequently passing overhead, I read a few poems to the main stage audience, including "For the Fifty (Who Made PEACE With Their Bodies)" (inspired by the "baring witness" demonstration) and two poems about air shows—Denise Levertov's "Air Show" and William Stafford's "Watching the Jet Planes Dive." Stafford's poem recalls his own struggle, as a conscientious objector during World War, to situate himself as a citizen in a country that no longer resembled itself; in *Down in My Heart*, Stafford's memoir of his years working and living in alternative service camps during the war, Stafford laments that "the country we had known was gone, had completely disappeared, was wiped out in a bombing that obliterated landmarks which had stood for years—since long before we were born."[11] Like the *lang/scape* poets, Stafford found himself an alien in his own land, attempting to re-map his surroundings by going back to "something forgotten by everyone alive."[12] The act Stafford describes involves sniffing out the earth for the scents that would bring us back home—the same metaphor that Susan Schultz employs to describe the poetic act. For Stafford, as for the *lang/scape* poets, "where roads are unconnected we must make a path."[13] Poems are signposts to find our collective way back.

"Blogging": From Hyperspace to People Space

Though the Internet has become a viable and even critical site for affiliation, information-gathering and archiving, and generating action for the peace movement, it is also a place whose labyrinthine spaces can rather look like democracy and yet remain invisible to the public. In a sinister way, the Internet—for all its utopian potential—can come to resemble the Matrix's version of the world; it looks real enough, but sometimes it has the uncanny feeling of a parallel, faux-universe. The Freeway Blogger (www.freewayblogger.com), who takes his *nom de guerre* from the exploding technology of weblogging and then applies it to actions in public spaces, has been working as an activist bringing pithy language into public spaces since 9/11. In particular, he has been placing signs on freeway overpasses and other very public spaces where the greatest number of people might see them, in his attempt to cut through the fog of mainstream media coverage. As you might imagine, many of the images and text tend to be blunt to the point of oversimplification and provocation.

But some invite a longer look, such as one the Freeway Blogger hung along a highway, consisting of three signs—"if this was / our policy," then an image of the so-called Abu Ghraib man, and then a third sign that read: "We're losing / a hell of a lot / more than just / a war."[14] I love the stanza (or poster) breaks and the line breaks. The colloquial language suddenly gathers symbolic resonance. "A hell of a lot" means "a lot" but it also evokes the hell that torture induces, a "lot" which we condemn ourselves by opening us up to future blowback and attacks. "More than just" both invokes and revokes the notion that torture can somehow be justified—the "just" evoking "not only," but also "justice" itself. What kind of "just war" can be invoked when "this" [torture] becomes part of the policy.

Yet even such language acts as a sign that reads "IMPEACH"—on a professor's door or highway overpass—however reductive or inflammatory, constitute an essential parallel intervention into the public conversation about this war. Though such signs may not necessarily succeed in "converting the unconverted," they nonetheless act as flickers of encouragement for those whose voices were left out of the discussion of this war. Online, his short video demo, "How to Reach 100,000 People for Under $1.00," shows him at work, and offers us the simple tools to make a freeway our page.[15]

The Sidewalk Blogger

Though I have argued that language acts such as the Freeway Blogger's are a kind of poetry, the Sidewalk Blogger actually is a well-known poet and publisher. Inspired by the Freeway Blogger, Sidewalk Blogger Susan Schultz demonstrates a poet's sense of brevity in her activist signage and her witty employment of public spaces and signage for her own textual production.[16] Bringing the disappeared language of the peace movement into public space in her environs of Kaneʻohe, Hawaiʻi, she regularly posts photographs of her work on Facebook, to share her narratives and images with those of us around the globe. Her project evolved, as she embraced new rhetorical angles, material for signage, and evolving contexts and narratives.

It began rather simply, with signs like the following: "BRING 'EM HOME ALIVE" painted bright red in bold letters, hung on a pedestrian overpass.

In addition to the images posted on Facebook, she includes short narratives that offer insight into her experience of hanging the signs at night—and then photographing them the following days. Here is what she wrote about the above picture:

> 9/3: left home just past 3 a.m. last night with the signs. The pedestrian overpass is on Kam Highway between town and the H3 off ramps. (The H3 goes to the Marine Corps Station in

one direction, Pearl Harbor in the other.) I put them up, but inside the white bars, because the wires I had were too short. Came home and asked B to cut me longer wires. Went back and moved the signs to the outside of the railing. When I entered my parking lot, just past 4 a.m., the property manager was starting his Ford SUV and when I got out of my car he was trolling the small parking lot. I think he shone his lights at me.[17]

These vignettes provide a window not only into the documentary photograph but also into the particular geographical and social landscape in which she finds herself. Hawai'i, after all, is the site not only of Pearl Harbor and all its historical associations but also of a number of large military bases. The vignette demonstrates the vulnerability of the Sidewalk Blogger to being exposed, even as she attempts to expose the war's effects on us: "I think he shone his lights at me."

The vulnerability of Sidewalk Blogger is replicated in the landscape as well—where there are other legible signs. In one image, she takes a wrecked car as her page, as if to suggest that the war itself is a car wreck, in which she placed a sign: "No War." Indeed, arguably every dollar that is spent on this war, inescapably, takes away money that could have been spent on children, infrastructure, our futures.

When I asked her to write more about her project, she explained that her

> project involves the hanging of signs on chain link fences on the windward side of O`ahu. This side of the island is a suburb to Honolulu; beyond the suburbs is what is left of country. My postal address is Kane'ohe, home of a large Marine Corps base from which many Marines are being shipped to Iraq. Hawai`i has over two dozen military bases in it [about 28]. The windward side of this island, while its politics are liberal—our congresswoman is Mazie Hirono, the only Buddhist in Congress—is fairly conservative. It's not rare to see cars with yellow ribbons, Standing Tall bumper stickers, and Hope Chapel adverts stuck on them.
>
> The purpose of the sign-hanging is to interrupt what my husband's cousin down the street calls "our communal apathetic hubris." Since most everyone on Oahu drives a car, of

necessity, signs are a way to get people's attention. My hero is the freeway blogger (freewayblogger.com) who does this in California. Different scale. So I call mine the Sidewalk Blog, though recently I've hung signs off pedestrian bridges over main roads. Also put up a roadside memorial to the dead, which is a way to engage the local culture of roadside memorials for car crash victims. And I have a new co-conspirator who is doing her best to put up more signs and memorials.

I have tried to incorporate humor (WAR STINKS on a sewage plant), but mainly to use the strategy of surprise and to write messages that are clear and short, like IMPEACH or NO WAR or OUT OF IRAQ.

I don't know what change such action effects, but it's all I can think to do. After seeing a young man arrested at a political meeting for asking a question at length, I suspect we need to use our right of free speech in order not to lose it.[18]

The Sidewalk Blogger sees her primary work as disrupting a collective "apathetic hubris," but her disruptions often involve humor and surprise. Such techniques often can hold at bay the reflex politicized judgment in the face of such play.

Another sign demonstrates her increasingly interactive approach with the environment; employing previously hung signs, she extends the "security" message "KEEP OUT" to an anti-war message: "KEEP OUT/of IRAN." The bold red letters in her piggyback sign invoke a humorous mimicry, one that saps the stentorian warning of the original sign, while communicating its own message.

As we entered the Advent season, the Sidewalk Blogger got the Christmas spirit and began targeting her Christian audience with a series of pointed questions about the relationship between Christianity and warfare. In preparation for a town Christmas parade, the Sidewalk Blogger went to work interpellating those who identify as Christians yet also maintain pro-war points of view. The proximity of the Knightcracker sign (a reference to the local Castle High School Knights) to the "Would Jesus Bomb?" sign places the two Christmases at odds with each other—the Christmas of warring rats and soldiers of "The Nutcracker," and the birth of Jesus.

Having inherited some old Christmas-themed signs, the Sidewalk Blogger produced some of her funniest and darkest anti-war propaganda. In the tradition of the IWW's *Little Red Book*, which provided radical lyrics for the tunes of traditional songs, The Sidewalk Blogger subverts the saccharine images of Santa and doe-eyed biblical figures with the language of protest. The Blogger transforms a cartoonish image of the Nativity—with Joseph and Mary kneeling before the baby Jesus in the manger, and the words "Come Let Us Adore Him"—into a message that reads "Come Let Us Impeach Him," with a smiling George W. Bush peering from the manger. Suddenly, Jesus and George W. Bush are conflated, but in ways that might not please the Christian Right. This sign disturbs because it forces us to confront how political power in the United States derives authority from its claims to fulfilling a Christian mission as "a light unto the nations."[19]

And next to a large banner publicizing a craft and gift fair (no doubt, to raise money for the public school), a Frosty the Snowman sign invites us to pay out millions per day to an unwinnable war: "Give to the Iraq War! $195 million per day!" Such juxtapositions provide a painful accounting of our national priorities as an imperial power. In the end, worldwide military dominance takes precedence over education. The Sidewalk Blogger's oscillation between satire and factuality offers the best sort of rhetorical one-two punch, since it offers its audience only a momentary relief of cynical distance before she draws the implications back home; in other words, we cannot laugh long when we begin to add up the costs—both personal and national—to us and to future generations.

Considered together, the Sidewalk Blogger's Christmas placards—with their cartoonish images of the winter holiday—are all the more striking against the backdrop of a semitropical Hawai'ian landscape that is both inside and outside the National Imaginary—that fantasy image that we have of ourselves. Hawai'i, one of the non-contiguous states, embodies the fantasy of expansion, of American colonial longing—part Gauguin's Tahiti, part Golf Course Heaven, part Dole's Pineapple Shangri-La. To place these "traditional" holiday signs in this landscape is to disrupt the very notion of a nation where everything is unified and the same. Such ephemeral markers that will last no longer than a day—perhaps even part of a day—nevertheless become, in their transience, images both of the tenuousness of historical memory and impermanence of arrogant power.

The Future of Poetry in Public Spaces

Lang/scape poets make a delible but visible mark on the landscape and, in the process, enable their readers to see their surroundings (both physical and political) in new ways. They have brought a new political materiality to poetry and a rhetorical nuance to the language of politics. Jules Boykoff and Kaia Sand, in *Landscapes of Dissent* (2008), called these poets "guerrilla poets"—poets operating on the edges of (or against) the law, whose page is public space itself, and whose readership is anyone who traverses those spaces. Amid the thicket of laws that govern and curtail free expression, guerrilla poets negotiate ways to appropriate public space from strictly commercial or privatized interests and attempt to render visible "the sharp edges of difference and inequality."[20] For these guerrilla poets, the language of resistance, and resistance through language, is *fertile*—insofar as it renders visible the voices that the presiding national narrative has repressed.

Boykoff and Sand make a strong argument for the "inadvertent" audience; even though public space can be a zone where isolatos pass through, locked between earbuds and cell screens—the old "lonely crowd" of sociological studies—it can also be a site where reading happens. Clearly, as the Sidewalk Blogger's experience shows, signs that called out "IM/PEACH" do not seem to last long in the landscape; they have been read, understood, and determined to be unfit for public consumption. Still, the inadvertent audience also may be the like-minded passerby who would receive these language interventions as mirrors of their unspoken or unheard thoughts. Which is to say: guerrilla poetry may succumb, in part, to the dangers of circular address; in other words, one might argue that their language interventions are principally for those already converted. Still, though we need a political poetry of conversion—that is to say, a poetry which hails those people who may not yet "know" the

132

narratives that might induce their resistance to a war or a political policy or an administration—we also need a poetry of provocation, of controversy, of confrontation. In the post-9/11 years, when the language of dissent itself had been disappeared, these guerrilla poets provided what amounted to a kind of public service, disseminating their own poetic versions of PSAs. After the quiescence of guerrilla poetry during the Obama age, the Trump presidency will, no doubt, provide ample occasion for a return to a wide range of dissident poetries—from *lang/scape* to guerrilla to page-based or performance/action work.

We live at a moment where not only poets, but all of us, risk limiting our rhetorical address to ourselves and those like ourselves. The digital echo chambers that led to Trump's election, and the surprise of the Left who did not see it coming, aptly demonstrate the problem. What *lang/scape* and guerrilla poets do, by making real the wars abroad and the violence at home, is to suture spaces in the public sphere where once the abyss of abstract political language existed. When the Sidewalk Blogger places the rising numbers of American soldiers dead in Iraq or when she juxtaposes the names of local cities and Iraqi cities, she participates in the critical act of what Fredric Jameson called "cognitive mapping"—that work of making visible the invisible relations between ourselves and others, at home and abroad.[21] Such poets challenge simultaneously the parochialism of our poetry and our politics, and provide a useful poetic "global positioning system" by which we might locate ourselves and where we need to go from here.

Since the original publication of this essay and *Landscapes of Dissent*, public poetry projects have proliferated, and even guerrilla tactics have become institutionalized; at the 2016 Split This Rock festival, for example, I walked the streets with dozens of other poets, distributing leaflet poems printed from the STR database, reading poems aloud on the streets of D.C. Some of us may have passed the bench at the DuPont Circle Metro stop, where E. Ethelbert Miller's elegy to the caretakers who lost loved ones during the AIDS epidemic is sculpted into the stone around a bench:

WE FOUGHT THE INVISIBLE
WE LOOKED TO ONE ANOTHER FOR COMFORT
WE HELD HANDS OF FRIENDS AND LOVERS
WE DID NOT TURN OUR BACKS
WE EMBRACED

The fact is that many of our public spaces—and, indeed, our digital spaces—have become saturated, reducing much language (whether ad-speak or poetry) to mere noise. Poems on subway cars bustle against advertisements for injury lawyers; sometimes, even, the adverts are more interesting than the poems. The debate around Banksy's guerrilla art on Israel's apartheid wall captures the dilemma. While his images demonstrate the nastiness of this wall and the longings of Palestinians to be free of it, they also make the wall also weirdly beautiful and paradoxically threaten to normalize its presence. The wall itself, for local Palestinians, is an atrocity, part of a further dispossession. Whatever is on it is mere decoration for colonization.

Some other *lang/scape* works, as in the art of Robert Montgomery, are hauntingly beautiful. One of Montgomery's "fire signs" (poetry installations set alight by a torch) that spells out "TO WAKE UP AND BE LIKE THE / WEATHER TO BE NO LONGER THE / BROKEN HEARTED SERVANTS / OF MAD KINGS" reads like a prescription for liberating oneself from tyranny. Yet more homely works can elicit an equally fierce response. Recently, when I drove beneath a bridge in a run-down neighborhood in Cleveland, I spied—to my delight—an anonymous poet's crooked-lettered poem: "THINK FOR YO SELF."

To wake up and be like the weather. To no longer be the broken-hearted servants of mad kings. To think for yo self. This is the call of poetry. It's why poets like Kaia Sand and E. J. McAdams have begun creating poetry walks, to learn to read the land again, to reclaim the unspoken histories of places, circling back to the twentieth century French Situationist practices not only of *détournement* (which lang/scape and guerrilla poetry also deploy) but also of *psychogeography*, the playful interaction with built spaces. Sand's *Remember to Wave* (2010) documents her own walks along the Columbia River in Portland, Oregon, a former site of Japanese internees, and occasioned other walks with participants to read that landscape together. E. J. McAdams, living and working in New York City, in his TRANSECTS project wanted to "figure out how 'outside' might collaborate on the poem . . . how one might engage the environment as a collaborator."[22] These poets remind us not only to see the landscape as palette or field for action but as collaborator and co-conspirator of our language, the con/text of all our poetic language, as we try to find a new way of telling the untold or unheard stories.

Notes

1. Jurgen Habermas, "The Public Sphere: An Encyclopedia Article (1964)," trans. Frank Lennox and Sara Lennox, in *New German Critique* 3 (1974), 49.

2. A. J. Liebling, "The Wayward Press: Do You Belong in Journalism?" *The New Yorker,* May 14, 1960, 109.

3. Philip Metres, *Behind the Lines: War Resistance Poetry on the American Homefront Since 1941* (Iowa City: University of Iowa Press, 2007), 223.

4. Philip Metres, "Poetry and the Peace Movement: Useable Pasts, Multiple Futures," *Big Bridge* 12 (2004), http://www.bigbridge.org/fictpmetres.htm

5. Susan Schultz, interview with Christine Thomas, "What I'm Reading: Susan Schultz," *The Honolulu Advertiser,* May 20, 2007, http://the.honoluluadvertiser.com/article/2007/May/20/il/FP705200356.html

6. Jurgen Habermas, "The Public Sphere," 49.

7. Ibid.

8. Donna Oehm Sheehan, "The Genesis of Our Peace Action," Baring Witness, accessed January 2, 2008, www.baringwitness.org/Genesis

9. Pau Reffell, "Baring Witness—The New Peace Movement," Baring Witness, accessed January 2, 2008, http://www.baringwitness.org/vision.htm

10. Jonathan LaGuardia, email to author, November 2007.

11. William Stafford, *Down in My Heart* (Swarthmore: Bench Press, 1985), 7.

12. William Stafford, "Watching the Jet Planes Dive," *The Way It Is: New and Selected Poems* (St. Paul: Graywolf, 1998), 68.

13. Ibid.

14. "Free Speech: Use It or Lose It," Freeway Blogger, accessed January 2, 2008, http://www.freewayblogger.com

15. *How To Reach 100,000 People for Under $1.00,* YouTube vid-

eo, 2:55, posted by Robert Corsini, https://www.youtube.com/watch?v=pFCL98m7Jeg

16. Images of the Sidewalk Blogger's work can be found embedded in the original version of this essay, at http://www.bigbridge.org/WAR-MET.HTM

17. Susan Schultz, email message to author, September 9, 2007.

18. Ibid.

19. Isaiah 49:6 NKJV.

20. Jules Boykoff and Kaia Sand, *Landscapes of Dissent: Guerrilla Poetry and the Politicization of Public Space* (Long Beach: Palm Press, 2008), 14.

21. Fredric Jameson, *Postmodernism, Or, The Cultural Logic of Late Capitalism* (Durham: Duke University Press, 1991), 409.

22. E. J. McAdams, interview by Philip Metres, *The Conversant,* April 17, 2013, http://theconversant.org/?p=3858

Installing Lev Rubinstein's
"Farther and Farther On"
From Note Cards to Field Walks

1.
Here, everything begins.
Everything begins here.
However, let's go farther.[1]

In *Close Listening: Poetry and the Performed Word* (1998), Charles Bernstein notes that "while the performance of poetry is as old as poetry itself, critical attention to modern and contemporary poetry performance has been negligible, despite the crucial importance of performance to the practice of poetry in this century."[2] Though some recent critical forays into poetry performance have begun to map the terrain, poetry performances, events, and stagings are still mostly unexplored.

2.
Here, no one will ask who you are and where you're from.
Everything is clear as is.
This is the place where you're spared persistent cross-examination.
But let's go farther.[3]

I'd like to investigate how the work of avant-garde Russian poet Lev Rubinstein—exemplified by the text "Farther and Farther On"—in its various print, dramatic, video, internet, and installation iterations—demonstrates the ways in which a "disembodied poetics" can signify once it moves through script to performance. By disembodied poetics, I mean to distinguish between two forms of poetry performance; in contrast to the slam trajectory of poetry performance, which demonstrates the vitality of the proximate and autobiographical body/text (body as text, text as body), the trajectory of "disembodied poetics" explicitly invites other bodies into coauthorship in ways that brings poetry into an active and changing multidimensionality.

8.
Here, one shouldn't stay for too long. Later it will probably become clear why.[4]

Like all of Rubinstein's poetic texts, which date from the early 1970s, "Farther and Farther On" was originally typed on the back of library catalogue cards, and read by the poet using the card as a temporal space. Each version of the text—book publications, a 2006 dramatic staging of the poem, and my multiple installations of the poem—poses this generative poem's possible significations, and points to the limits of each iteration—shifting us both backward in time and forward again, into its multiple futures.

12.
Here it's written: "Passerby: Stop. Think."[5]

13.
The next inscription reads: "Passerby: Stop. Try to think of something better than that."[6]

My first experience of the avant-garde was through the Russian conceptualist movement, when I began reading and interviewing Russian poets in Moscow in 1992 and 1993. Vsevolod Nekrasov, a leading conceptualist of the Lianozovo group in Moscow, regaled with stories of how artists would get together and make "everyday life" the material of art:

> A bunch of people could get together and drive to the countryside, not because they decided to take a walk in the fresh air, and not because they want to create a work of art. And our motivation would be unclear, like "hey let's go and see what happens." And nothing will happen. It'll be just a few people in a peaceful place.

So the object is an action, an attempt to create something. And the attempt is not premeditated, because if it is premeditated it will be boring. For example, there's a field about 300 meters across and a forest nearby. In the middle of the field is a table; on the table are ten poles, and on each pole is a spool; on each spool is a string. So we pull the string and go. And along the way unreel the string. Everyone goes like *burlaki* [boat-haulers] pulling a boat over a dry river. In the forest there's less snow, you can go out onto some road. You see, there are no obligations. You can decide not to reel and go back to the station. I would rather go to the station because the road is already close. Some other people show up and other things happen. There's no artistic, esthetic, extraordinary moment. It's just something colloquial, constructed with natural curiosity. Unwind, unwind and see what will happen.

Another time we met at Sokolniki Park. We walked a long time and wondered: when will the action begin? The action actually already was happening. Behind us people were walking with tape recorders, taping our conversations, our passing comments. It turned out that we were the artists, we made something. In that way, reality is the most valuable, richest material. And at the same time, the most familiar. Conceptualism is not the art of realism, but the art of reality.[7]

What Nekrasov proposed was a kind of art that would be almost indistinguishable from life—an avant-garde not of provocation but of the everyday. Still, in 1974, the infamous "Bulldozer Exhibition" occurred, when an open air avant-garde exhibition of Lianozovo artists was literally bulldozed by Soviet police.

18.
Let's go farther.[8]

Around this time, Lev Rubinstein made his own leap through conceptualist practices to a poetry that has been called "postmodern Chekhov." Born in 1947, Rubinstein worked for many years as a librarian in Moscow's Lenin Library. The legend is that, like Dr. William Carlos Williams and his prescription pad, Rubinstein just needed something to write on. Yet handling and cataloguing books for a living gave Rubinstein a keen awareness of the materiality of texts—their constructedness, their boundedness by genre, author, and geometry. In other words, surrounded by books, Rubinstein discovered a poetic method to release himself from the prison of the printed page.

> 19.
> *Here someone in the half-darkness decides to part with hope and*
>   *cannot;*
> *Someone, finding himself in financial difficulty, looks for a way out*
>   *and cannot find one;*
> *Someone tries to draw a distinct line between what is past and what*
>   *is to come. He just isn't noticed;*
> *Someone worked it out so that everything he says fits the situation.*
>   *People like this. He is noticed . . .*[9]

When his generation finally emerged into the post-Soviet public eye, and the time came that publishers wanted to reproduce his work, Rubinstein allowed publishers to reprint his work in book form. In Rubinstein's preface to the first anthology version, Rubinstein asks the reader to recall that "the text in the form of note cards is the original, and its 'flat' variant is closer to a copy, a reproduction. Or, more precisely, a photograph of a sculpture."[10] In another introduction, "What Can I Say?" Rubinstein writes that "the authentic—that is the 'spatial'—variant of my text is related to its flat (book) version in approximately the same way as, for example, an orchestral score relates to a rendition for one or two instruments."[11] In both introductions, though, he adds a tentative note, that "the author's version is itself just a version."[12]

> 20.
> *Here someone over-attentive doesn't notice the most important thing.*
>   *Concentrating on tiny details, he looks a little silly;*
> *Someone striving for eternity slips and falls. A bright light falls on*
>   *him. It's quite a pitiful sight;*
> *Someone is unable to come to his senses from some dumbfounding*
>   *news. So he just goes on living, stunned;*
> *Someone loses himself in the crowd. They discover him, greet him*
>   *noisily, almost by force drag him out to the middle. And there he*
>   *stands;*[13]

In 2006, James Tyson, the Theatre Programmer of Chapter Arts in Wales, directed a dramatic staging of "Farther" after reading the translation and, in his words, "was immediately drawn to it as a piece which spoke about the theatre, and the multiple voices, of past and present that can coexist within the theatre."[14] Using the whole text, Tyson and the two performers wanted "that text, almost as an object, to coexist on the stage with the two performers."[15] Tyson's fascinating staging proves the strengths of the stage in embodying voices and voicing embodiments, but it also shows the stage's limits for Rubinstein's disembodied poetics; since its generativity is grounded precisely in its lack of a singular locus of voice (or even two voices), and since it is at once a gathering and dispersal of voices, Rubinstein's "Farther" on stage became literalized when the director chose to have all the lines read by two characters alone, thus limiting the chorale effect of the text.

28.
Let's go farther.[16]

Since "Farther and Farther On" invites spatialization, I've experimented with installing the poem in homage to the Lianozovo conceptualists. Concluding two courses on poetry, I created an installation of "Farther" consisting of small cards following Rubinstein's order, which I attached in the ground on an open grassy quad at John Carroll University. Beginning at a landmark—a huge bust of John Carroll—I invited students in small groups from the classroom to walk through the installation. It curved around the three-fourths of the quad, not completing the circle but ending close enough that they could return to the bust for the conclusion of class.

Watching them go through the installation and watching others watch them, I was struck by how creating the texts as small as they were, the students would have to lean over or even kneel in the grass, every ten feet or so, to read another card. It created this odd effect, whereby it looked as if they were bowing to the ground.

I was happy that other things were happening on the quad— some guys were hitting some golf balls, another class sat in a circle, etc.—which created this feeling of art and life existing simultaneously. Other students, in fact, started reading some of the cards, at times midway through, which must have made little sense, or a completely new sense. What surprised me most about the reaction to the text was how it resonated for graduating seniors as a kind of invitation to think about what confronted them after the bounds of college, *farther on.*

31.
Here it's said: "All those guilty without sin, those bitten and shy,
those intently pondering and those attracted by a barely-audible
voice of eternity, those stooped from the backbreaking puzzles of
existence, those in undue agitation from God knows what news,
those anxiously listening to what is said—where do they find
themselves heading?"[17]

In 2007, at the University of Louisville's literature conference, I had a chance to videotape my panel audience as they did a walking-reading of the text in a chilly morning in February and document the experience. First, once the participants knew they were going to be reading, the whole landscape became charged with possible meanings. Lynn Keller gestured to a tossed-away piece of paper on the ground, wondering if it was part of the installation. It was just a piece of paper, and I said so. Everyone in the group burst out laughing, and Alan Golding noted: "every sign is a sign."[18]

35.
Another voice: "Well just imagine, with that smile of his he just
walked through all this hell. He's a very unique human being.
I've never seen anyone like him in my entire life . . ."[19]

36.
Another voice: "By the way, he also can't stand her. So you really
shouldn't . . ."[20]

The writing was so small, that people had to bow or kneel to the text in the grass. Mike Magee bent down from his waist, as if to royalty. Somewhere in the middle of the journey, Kaplan Harris noted during the middle of the text that there were "a lot of someones."[21] Barrett Watten concurred, saying, "it's getting pretty complicated. Someone's got to be doing a lot of work."[22] (I like having video evidence that Barrett Watten is kvetching that someone's text is making him work.) Later, Watten waxed Marxist: "What is further? Communism is further. That's the point. It's not there yet. We're not at communism yet. We're being directed to it. Sure, we're going to communism."[23]

Watten's complaint aside, people seemed to love this walk in the field, to move slowly through the installation. Some didn't wish it would end. Chris Green stopped for a moment, saying, "I feel so good, if I finish I might not feel so good."[24] Lynn Keller, Carla Harryman, Alan Golding, and Dee Morris took the longest, and demonstrated what I noted to them as obsessive close reader habits. Alan Golding quipped, "close readers of a close reading."[25]

Upon completing the fifty-two-card series, Chris Green reflected: "here's the deal. I used to spend so many nights walking around the streets, without a reason to go anyplace, just to walk. These little cards are the voices I hear. Now, locked in a job, we have to have an impetus to find our voices again."[26] Jessica Lewis Luck liked how the installation made us "bring the brain and body around" the movement and the reading at the same time.[27]

47.
Scene: The dacha at night. The trains sound their horns, husky in the distance. It's very cold.[28]

My own initial reader experience of the text was of wonder and awe, much like the Russian conceptualists inventing their new forms in the parks around Moscow. "Farther and Farther On," in its parodies of public signage, felt both utopian and dystopian at the same time, as one shifts from the initial innocent desire to keep moving to set pieces in which "someones" find themselves in awkward or even terrifying spaces; here, the poem turns into a Dantesque rendering of the suffering of solitary individuals; then, the poem begins to hear and set voices against each other, followed by some rather Biblical pronouncements, only to end with stage settings in the mode of Chekhov.

Watten's offhand comment about the Soviet allusions of "Farther" added another layer. In the Soviet imagination, the language and iconography of forward movement, of progress, is so embedded that the early cards of the poem could not but evoke that cultural specificity, even as it challenged and evacuated it of its political meanings. The Stagnation Period of the late 1970s and early 1980s, when Rubinstein was writing, was at once a time of political cynicism and one in which the Soviet Union seemed as if it might never end. Exposing the emptiness of the language of progress was a deeply political gesture, even though the goal, to my mind, was not resistance alone. It was to create another way of being.

Installing "Farther" momentarily liberated the text from authorial intention and its cultural/historical matrices and also accrued new ones based on the site and the readers involved. This brings me to my final thoughts on the avant-garde of the American variety. The American avant-garde often has articulated its goals through poetics statements and manifestos, which simultaneous crystallize and threaten to ossify the work itself, creating new demands that younger generations of poets could not fail to resist. Re-staging Rubinstein offered me a way out of a poetics that have occasionally attempted to freeze the possible meanings of work. Perhaps, now, we ought to see such manifestos and poetics as signposts along the way to a heretofore-incompleted poesis.

51.

Another scene: A veranda, fragrant with flowers of fruit trees. Two
*   swings. One swing lightly rocks: it's clear that someone just*
*   got off it. Offstage, voices: an agitated female one, a calming*
*   male one. No one has appeared on stage yet. Sounds of nearing*
*   thunder. It suddenly darkens.*[29]

Notes

1. Lev Rubinstein, *Compleat Catalogue of Comedic Novelties,* trans. Philip Metres and Tatiana Tulchinsky (Brooklyn: Ugly Duckling Presse, 2014), 3.

2. Charles Bernstein, introduction to *Close Listening: Poetry and the Performed Word* (New York: Oxford University Press, 1998), 3.

3. Rubinstein, op.cit., 3.

4. Ibid., 4.

5. Ibid., 4.

6. Ibid., 4.

7. Philip Metres, "Vsevolod Nekrasov with Philip Metres," *The Conversant*, 2014. http://theconversant.org/?p=2864

8. Rubinstein, op.cit., 5.

9. Ibid., 5.

10. Ibid., xxiv.

11. Ibid., xiv.

12. Ibid., xxiv.

13. Ibid., 5.

14. James Tyson, Chapter Arts Centre website, original article no longer accessible.

15. Ibid.

16. Rubinstein, op. cit., 12.

17. Ibid., 8.

18. Alan Golding, in discussion with the author, February 2007.

19. Rubinstein, op. cit., 9.

20. Ibid.

21. Kaplan Harris, in conversation with the author, February 2007.

22. Barrett Watten, in conversation with the author, February 2007.

23. Ibid.

24. Chris Green, in conversation with the author, February 2007.

25. Alan Golding, op. cit.

26. Chris Green, op. cit.

27. Jessica Lewis Luck, in conversation with the author, February 2007.

28. Rubinstein, op. cit., 11.

29. Rubinstein, op. cit., 11.

Against a Cloistered Virtue
Poems for Peace

In May 2009, in a backyard in Portland, Oregon, a few poets and artists who had come for the "Another World Instead: William Stafford Peace Symposium" found themselves possessed by what appeared to be a simple question posed by Kim Stafford: If we were to suggest bookstores carry a "peace shelf," what would should it carry?

As dusk fell, I scribbled furiously as Jeff Gundy, Fred Marchant, Paul Merchant, Haydn Reiss, Kim, and I widened the shelf, until it was a bookcase, and it seemed that we'd need a whole store; and later on via email, when Sarah Gridley joined the conversation, we probed a concept that teeters between immensely practical and dangerously amorphous: How to canonize a list of texts that envision a more just and peaceful world—for bookstores, for teachers, for interested readers—without turning it into Borges' "Library of Babel," which contains every book ever written?

And how to overcome—in ourselves, in the poetry world, and in all the communities in which we situate ourselves—our own resistances to an engaged poetry that stakes specific claims about the world, a poetry that could be partisan and provocative and even utopian? After all, many feel as Keats did, that "We hate poetry that has a palpable design upon us—and if we do not agree, seems to put its hand in its breeches pocket. Poetry should be great and unobtrusive, a thing which enters into one's soul, and does not startle or amaze with itself, but with its subject."[1]

And if the poetry that presses "palpable design upon us" were not challenge enough, then what to do about poetry that proposes something about peace, the very word of which seems lost in a ganja haze and lacks the pungency of real life; or, to let Keats twitter on the subject, "for axioms in philosophy are not axioms until they are proved upon our pulses."[2] Ezra Pound's Imagiste manifesto similarly exhorts poets to avoid abstractions: "Don't use such an expression as 'dim lands of peace.' It dulls the image. It mixes an abstraction with the concrete. It comes from the writer's not realizing that the natural object is always the adequate symbol."[3]

Our lexicon for peacemaking is poor not because we have no experience of peace or peacemaking, but because the language of violence and war has been ubiquitous in our culture, and enormously profitable for those in power. And with the mightiest military in the history of the world, in perhaps the most adaptable empire, we live under conditions that Paul Virilio, borrowing from William James, calls *Pure War*—a state in which the endless preparation for war constitutes the real war. We need to realize the dim lands of peace, however dim they may seem at first. (We live them and know them, in moments. And more than moments.) Though our poetry has ably represented the traumatic and unmaking operations of war—from the rage of Achilles on to our present—it has also often unwittingly glorified and perpetuated a culture of war. We have yet to give adequate attention to how our poetry also contains the seeds of other ways of dealing with conflict, oppression, and injustice, and how it may advance our thinking into what a future without war might look like.

If "peace" seems abstract, foggy, weak, and utopian, it is also a problem of language. The word *peace* has rich etymological roots, from the Latin *pacem*, and related to the Greek *eirene*, which was used by translators to evoke the Hebrew word "shalom," meaning peace, welfare, and prosperity. *Pax* meant a "treaty of peace, tranquility, absence of war," and peace appeared in the twelfth century in Anglo-Norman as "freedom from civil disorder," was related to the word "fasten," and replaced the Old English term which also meant "happiness." The notion of "peace of mind" dates from the thirteenth century. Peace is not merely the absence of war but the presence of positive social, ecological, and spiritual relations. To these definitions, we should add Gandhi's notion of *satyagraha* (truth force) or what Levertov calls in her poem "Making Peace"—"an energy field more intense than war."[4] To use A. J. Muste's phrase, echoing Buddhist and Taoist teachings: "There is no way to peace. Peace is the way."[5]

How to imagine peace, how to make peace? In our conversations on the Peace Shelf, three general categories emerged: Sorrows, Resistance, and Alternative Visions. It's simple enough: we need to witness the horrors of war, we need to resist and find models of resistance, and we need to imagine and build another world. We cannot get to peace without imagining and building another world, but we cannot have peace at all if we don't confront the reality of war and conflict, and what is in us that leans toward violence. Poetry has been there, since the beginnings of human history, its violent leanings and peaceful longings.

From the beginning, poetry and the quest for peace have been intertwined, since the first known poet Enheduanna's laments against war. There is something in us that recoils against violence, against the culture of militarism and heroism that aid and abet mass organized violence. Nearly four thousand years ago, in "Lament to the Spirit of War," the Sumerian priestess Enheduanna bemoans war: "Like a fiery monster you fill the land with poison. / As thunder you growl over the earth, / trees and bushes collapse before you."[6] In Enheduanna's hands, war is personified, a monstrous presence born of "hate, greed, and anger," who wreaks destruction on both humanity and nature. "Who can explain," the poem ends, "why you go on so?"[7] We're still asking that question. During the 2003 Iraq War, Iraqi poet Dunya Mikhail would write her own poem personifying war, "The War Works Hard," wryly praising its industry and eagerness, how it "contributes to the industry / of artificial limbs . . . [and] invigorates the coffin makers."[8]

Perhaps the first punk, the Greek poet Archilochus, thumbing his nose at the tradition of dying honorably:

Well, what if some barbaric Thracian glories
in the perfect shield I left under a bush?
I was sorry to leave it—but I saved my skin.
Does it matter? Oh hell, I'll buy a better one.[9]

Spartan women were wont to tell their men going off to war to hold onto their shields; "with it or on it" became the terse saying that meant, I'll only want to see you victorious and with your shield or dead with dignity. Archilochus tweaks such heroism. Take that, Sparta.

A few hundred years after Archilochus, the Greek poet Sappho praises love over weaponry in her "Anactoria Poem": "Some say thronging cavalry, some say foot soldiers, / others call a fleet the most beautiful of / sights the dark earth offers, but I say it's what- / ever you love best."[10] Alongside Aristophanes' play *Lysistrata*, in which the fed-up women of Greece withhold sex to try to end the Peloponnesian War, Sappho's poem explicitly rejects the idea that war is beautiful. Like the ancient Greeks, the 1960s counterculture also proclaimed it: *Make love, not war.*

As these ancient poems show, peace poetry isn't just sweetness and light. "Peace" is no mere cloud-bound dream, but a dynamic of dealing with conflict, oppression, and hatred without either resigning ourselves to violence or seizing into our own violent response; peace poems vividly and demonstrably articulate and embody such a way. At their best, peace poems, as John Milton did in "Aereopagitica," argue against "a fugitive and cloistered virtue, unexercised and unbreathed, that never sallies out and sees her adversary."[11] If, in Milton's words, "that which purifies us is trial, and trial is by what is contrary,"[12] then peace poetry must also interrogate the easy pieties of the peace movement and its own ideological blind spots. And indeed, Michael True's exploration of nonviolent literature confirms that "although writings in [the nonviolent tradition] resemble conventional proclamations recommending peace reform, their tone and attitude tend to be provocative, even disputatious, rather than conciliatory."[13]

What follows is a selection of poems from *Come Together: Imagine Peace* (2008) that point to the dynamics of peace poetry, beginning with William Stafford. Stafford, a conscientious objector during the Second World War, emerged as perhaps the most important American *pacifist* poet. Though peace poetry is not limited to pacifists or pacifism, Stafford's deceptively simple poems were concerned with confronting the problem of violence and the breakdown of human community from an explicitly nonviolent, but not doctrinaire, perspective. It's not a mistake that the poem for which he is best known, the ecologically-minded "Traveling through the Dark," may well be one of the best poems about World War II—engaging the question of whether killing, particularly the killing of innocents, can ever be justified.

Unlike most of Stafford's poems, which hail the reader with a nonpartisan voice, "Peace Walk" actively embodies the collective "we" as a group of war resisters on an "un-march." The poem represents a peace walk that defies the conventions of protest as a noisy and antagonistic rabble. It begins with uncertainty: "we wondered what our walk should mean,"[14] as those on the walk bear the stares and othering by fellow citizens: "like an elevator going down, their look at us."[15] This is how the poem ends:

> Above our heads the sound truck blared—
> by the park, under the autumn trees—
> it said that love could fill the atmosphere:
>
> Occur, slow the other fallout, unseen,
> on islands everywhere—fallout, falling
> unheard. We held our poster up to shade our eyes.
>
> At the end we just walked away;
> no one was there to tell us where to leave the signs.[16]

Though the poem clearly walks along with the demonstrators, it vibrates with ambiguity and self-critique. Stafford self-effacingly points to the limits of the demonstrators' vision (both physical and metaphorical) and of the walk itself; "we held our poster up to shade our eyes" suggests both a desire to flee the protest and the judging gaze of the bystanders.

Despite the fact that any ideological placard narrows a person's perception, Stafford does not condemn the demonstration or demonstrators; in fact, the final lines contain in their lonely description of the protest's dispersal a vision of egalitarian society. It would be easy to read the final couplet simply as the failure of the demonstration, of Stafford's poetic skepticism of a public protest. Yet, the fact that "no one was there to tell us where to leave the signs" compels the individual demonstrators, and not some organizer, to decide what to do with the "signs"—

not just the physical placards but also the things that they signify: the dangers of nuclear testing, the resistance to warfare, a vision of the beloved community.

In the debate carried out in letters between Robert Duncan and Denise Levertov during the Vietnam War, the general consensus among contemporary poets and critics is that Duncan was right. That consensus, it seems to me, is to our loss. The debate itself is the thing. The argument between a poetry that favors the aesthetic, the formal, and the individual, and a poetry that favors the political, the rhetorical, and the cultural-political movement suggests the ongoing and necessarily provisional rapprochement between artistic production and the peace movement. They represent not an unbridgeable impasse between politics and poetry but an ongoing negotiation over how poetry's particular power might best bear witness to and serve a culture of resistance.

The truth is that neither Duncan nor Levertov wrote their best work about or against the Vietnam war. Yet Levertov's intimate relationship to the peace movement bears particular attention, even admiration: "'Tell Denise to wear a helmet,' Joe Dunn wrote from Boston: 'she's our Joan of Arc and we can't afford to lose her' . . . Denise Levertov has put her life over there on the picket line."[17]

In "Making Peace" (1987), Levertov revisits what motivated her resistance to the Vietnam War and answers the criticism of her anti-war poetry, which Duncan and others saw as a failure of poetry and a failure of vision. Yet, here she resists relying on an ideological plan:

> But peace, like a poem,
> is not there ahead of itself,
> can't be imagined before it is made,
> can't be known except
> in the words of its making,
> grammar of justice,
> syntax of mutual aid.[18]

Levertov's definitional probing proposes, like A. J. Muste's saying, that peace is not an end, it is a way, and that to prescribe a certain vision of the possible might be to proscribe what may need to unfold. Peace is not defined by an absence of war. It's an energy field, something vibrating with an invisible but palpable power, marked by the "grammar of justice, / syntax of mutual aid." No justice, no interdependence, no peace. If we "restructure the sentence our lives are making,"[19] then we might have peace:

> an energy field more intense than war,
> might pulse then,
> stanza by stanza into the world,
> each act of living
> one of its words . . .[20]

I love the way in which she makes the poem the work of peace, and the work of peace into a poem, composed of our lives as words. I'm less convinced by her concluding image of a forming crystal; that, too, is the problem of peacebuilding. Our metaphors stretch and reach to something that may be beyond language. Our vision fails. Yet we keep reaching.

Peace poetry—like the peace movement itself—is not limited to white Boomer liberals singing along with John Lennon's "Imagine." Courageous and outspoken poets like African American poet Audre Lorde helped bring the peace movement back home, into the streets and courtrooms and bedrooms, and widened the occasionally limited vision of what war looks like and what peace might require. Written in response to the not guilty verdict of a police officer who killed a ten-year-old boy (in which a single black woman of the jury was "convinced" by the eleven white men), Lorde's "Power" casts the stakes of poetry in starkly violent terms, at the outset:

> The difference between poetry and rhetoric
> is being
> ready to kill
> yourself

instead of your children.
I am trapped on a desert of raw gunshot wounds
and a dead child dragging his shattered black
face off the edge of my sleep[21]

In Lorde's recalibration of Yeats' distinction between poetry and
rhetoric, poetry is a kind of self-murder, insofar as it calls one to
be ready to sacrifice the self for the sake of the future. The line
breaks exacerbate the tension between violence against another
and against oneself—and suggest that these kinds of violence
are intimately connected. Lorde is haunted by the killing of this
young black boy, and she is haunted by her response to it, trying to find within herself not a desire to forgive but a desire to
survive with her humanity intact.

The policeman who shot down a 10-year-old in Queens
stood over the boy with his cop shoes in childish blood
and a voice said "Die you little motherfucker" and
there are tapes to prove that. At his trial
this policeman and in his own defense
"I didn't notice the size or nothing else
only the color." and
there are tapes to prove that, too.
Today that 37-year-old white man with 13 years of police
    forcing
has been set free
by 11 white men who said they were satisfied
justice had been done
and one black woman who said
"They convinced me" meaning
they had dragged her 4'10" black woman's frame
over the hot coals of four centuries of white male approval
until she let go the first real power she ever had
and lined her own womb with cement
to make a graveyard for our children.[22]

The trial becomes a second killing; not only does the child's
death slip away without justice, but a black woman is required
to sacrifice her own power to white male supremacy. Lorde's desire to overcome her own self-protection—just as she wished the
single black juror had, to stand up for the sacredness of that mur-

dered child—requires her to access her own destructive impulses and, in her words, "to use / the difference between poetry and rhetoric" to be able to live without hating every white person.

The great anti-war poems written by soldiers have often confronted war with frank honesty, sometimes bitter anger, and great compassion for war's victims. Yet too often, the soldier's own victimization has tended to efface the civilian victims, who have come to bear the costs of war disproportionately. By contrast, Wislawa Szymborska's "The End and the Beginning" lends a sympathetic civilian-eye view of the battlefield, where unphotographed "someones" must clean up the rubble churned up by mass violence. I love the opening tone of this poem, which captures the annoyed mother-voice that we might do well to obey more fervently.

> After every war
> someone has to clean up.
> Things won't
> straighten themselves up, after all.
>
> Someone has to push the rubble
> to the sides of the road,
> so the corpse-laden wagons
> can pass.[23]

The poet captures what happens when "the cameras have left / for another war," the survivors who have to rebuild a world:

> Someone, broom in hand,
> still recalls how it was.
> Someone listens
> and nods with unsevered head.[24]

Is there any more starkly surreal description of survivors in poetry that one who "nods with unsevered head"?

Despite the surreal phantasmagoria of such a line, the poem's final image is that of a person lying peacefully in the grass, looking up at the sky, in utter relaxation:

In the grass which has overgrown
reasons and causes,
someone must be stretched out
blade of grass in his mouth
gazing at the clouds.[25]

What would peace look like for Israel/Palestine? For years, I've been teaching a course on the literature of the Israeli-Palestinian conflict, exploring how the literature not only dramatizes the human realities and costs of this protracted conflict but also proposes possible solutions. If war is a failure of the imagination, in the words of William Blake, then visionary language has a role to play in ending war.

Yehuda Amichai, the greatest Israeli poet, whose poems carry a wounded tenderness, speaks for the Jewish nation in a way that often surpasses the boundaries of national identity. In "Wildpeace," this former soldier searches for a way to describe what peace would be for him, but it is not a political or Biblical vision:

Not the peace of a cease-fire
not even the vision of the wolf and the lamb,
but rather
as in the heart when the excitement is over
and you can talk only about a great weariness.[26]

He proceeds through the negative, rejecting different kinds of peace: the peace of the military cease-fire, and the peace of the apocalyptic prophetic verse, "the big noise of beating swords into plowshares" (Isa. 11: 6–7 NIV). Rather, he explores peace as a feeling after a "great weariness," something that is evanescent, light, floating, lazy like foam. There are heartbreaking lines in this poem that register the world through a soldier's eyes: "I know I know how to kill, / that makes me an adult."[27] In the end, he proposes that it must be natural, and the ground must be ready for it:

Let it come
like wildflowers,
suddenly, because the field
must have it: wildpeace.[28]

155

What is most painful to me about this beautiful poem is to know that its author, in fighting for his new state's independence, also played a role in the active dispossession of Palestinians and the destruction of hundreds of Palestinian villages in 1948–49. Sometimes poems are wiser than their writers. I often think of his "The Place Where We Are Right" as a poem that says what he and some Israelis have never been able to admit, in which "the place where we are right / is hard and trampled / like a yard."[29] That poem ends:

> But doubts and loves
> dig up the world
> like a mole, a plough.
> And a whisper will be heard in the
> place
> where the ruined
> house once stood.[30]

While the poem never explicitly references what Palestinians call "*Nakba*," the catastrophe of 1948, in which over four hundred Arab villages were wiped off the map, it can be read as a stark admonishment of blinkered nationalism that would tear up the planet for "doubts and loves."

Born in Birwe in 1942 and exiled to Lebanon in 1948 during the war, when Birwe was destroyed, Mahmoud Darwish became the poet laureate of the Palestinian people and exiles throughout the world from a young age, receiving wide acclaim for such early poems as the blistering "Identity Card" and the bittersweet elegy "My Mother." Early Darwish embodied what Ghassan Kanafani and Barbara Harlow have termed "resistance poetry"—explicitly political writing conceived as a force for mobilizing resistance and acting as a repository of national consciousness. Yet the full range of his work—from the stark social realism of "Identity Card" to the visionary mode of "We Travel Like Other People"—resists any easy reduction of Darwish to "resistance poet."

A State of Siege, the book-length poem written during the beginning of the Second Intifada and the siege of Ramallah in 2002, ranks among the great political long poems in recent memory, in the tradition of Anna Akhmatova's *Requiem*. Like the best political poems, *A State of Siege* succeeds because it moves beyond protest into a richly polyvocal rumination of the psychology of siege—the siege of bodies and consciousnesses alike. It summons the voices of the neutral, the outraged, future bombers, and victims, one after another. It's as if we're in a crowd caught in crossfire. The poem's focused glimpses enables those of us privy only to the soul-crushing images of street beatings and rock throwers to have a glimpse inside, as it were, to the subjective tremors of being that such upheaval inevitably cause:

> When the fighter planes disappear, the doves fly
> white, white. Washing the sky's cheek
> with free wings, reclaiming the splendor and sovereignty
> of air and play. Higher and higher
> the doves fly, white white. I wish the sky
> were real (a man passing between two bombs told me)[31]

The war creates a feeling that the heavens and its broad possibilities are foreclosed, fictional, unreal. Darwish (rendered through the brilliant assonant-rich translation of Fady Joudah) juxtaposes the classic image of the peaceful dove with the benumbed mutterings of a passerby, working his way outside between attacks.

Yet Darwish's poem holds fast to its own humane vision, where no one is unworthy of living. Consider the following fragment, spoken by a Palestinian:

> You standing at the doorsteps, enter
> and drink Arabic coffee with us
> (you might sense you're human like us)
> you standing at the doorsteps of houses,
> get out of our mornings,
> we need reassurance that we
> are human like you!

In this comic moment, Darwish captures the painful dehumanization of the siege—how it saps the soul of both the occupier and the occupied, each diminished and shorn of their humanity.

Darwish's poem also engages in speculative thinking, in ways that reminded me of Amichai's "The Diameter of the Bomb," which proposes that the bomb's ripple effects are more than the feet that its shrapnel extends but includes all the victims of victims who suffer the loss of their loved ones:

> (To another killer:) Had you left the fetus
> for thirty days, the possibilities would have changed:
> the occupation might end and that suckling
> would not remember the time of siege,
> and he'd grow up a healthy child, become a young man
> and study in the same institution with one of your daughters
> the ancient history of Asia
> and they might fall together in passion's net
> and beget a girl (and she'd be Jewish by birth)
> so what have you done then?
> Now your daughter has become a widow
> and your granddaughter an orphan?
> What have you done to your fugitive family
> and how did you strike three doves with one shot?[32]

I'm reminded of Mother Theresa's well-known aphorism: "If we don't have peace, that's because we have forgotten we belong to each other." In the end, as another fragment from the poem proposes, the moral imagination invites us to include the other in our web of human relationships:

> "Me, or him"
> that's how war starts. But
> it ends in an awkward stance:
> "Me and him"[33]

I could write a book just on this poem, but what makes this a peace poem is that it moves from a catalogue of loss to a litany for peace. By the end, echoing Amichai's "Wildpeace," Darwish predicts that "This siege will extend until / the besieger feels, like the besieged, / that boredom / is a human trait."[34] Ending with a litany of "Salaams," Darwish's poem moves through the resistance of the freedom fighter (*muquwama*) and steadfast resistance of the civilian (*sumud*) toward something like a vision of future coexistence between Israelis and Palestinians:

Salaam is two enemies, longing, each separately,
to yawn on boredom's sidewalk

Salaam is two lovers moaning to bathe
in moonlight . . .

Salaam is a train that unites all its passengers
who are coming from or going to a picnic in eternity's
    suburbs . . .

Salaam is the public confession of truth:
What have you done with the murdered's ghost?

Salaam is the turning toward an errand in the garden:
What will we plant in a little while?[35]

In the midst of occupation and siege, Darwish maintains his empathic vision. He knows that life isn't permanent, and that this salaam is a train that unites us all in our journey toward eternity. He knows that *salaam* demands patience. That when we plant "in a little while," we plant for a future harvest.

Israeli poet Aharon Shabtai was known first for his translations and then for his erotic verse, and then for the excoriating protest of *J'Accuse*. Like the Hebrew prophets who attacked the nation and advocated for the oppressed, Shabtai has relished his role as anti-Zionist gadfly. In "Lotem Abdel Shafi," Shabtai attacks the separation barrier between Israel and the West Bank:

The heart dies without space for love, without a moral
    horizon:
think of it then as a bird trapped in a box.
My heart goes out with love to those beyond the fence;
only toward them can one really advance, that is, make
    progress.
Without them I feel I'm half a person.[36]

Citing the example of "Romeo and Juliet," Shabtai proposes (as parable) the marriage of his daughter to a prominent Palestinian family. In "Lotem Abdel Shafi"—the name his daughter would have if she married into the family of well-known Palestinian Haidar Abdel Shafi—Shabtai echoes *Iphigenia at Aulis* as he proposes a classically comedic solution to the conflict. In the act of union, he imagines:

> The Arab groom from Gaza, too, will extend to my daughter
> a dress
> on which is embroidered the Land redeemed from
> Apartheid's curse—
> our Land as a whole, belonging equally to all of its
> offspring.[37]

If there's one poet who assumed the mantle of William Stafford, it's the Palestinian-American poet Naomi Shihab Nye. Like Stafford, Nye often writes in an approachable style whose surface clarity belies the complex currents within. As importantly, Nye's poetry embraces the tough conciliatory spirit—steely in its commitment to openness and generosity—that marked Stafford's life and work. While peace poetry may occasionally provoke, it also must dramatize the sometimes tentative, sometimes outlandish reaching across the abyssal distances between antagonists. Nye's "Jerusalem," quoted in full earlier, addresses the conflict at the heart of the holy city by naming our fundamental woundedness, a pain that often leads us to lash out: "each carries a tender spot: / something our lives forgot to give us."[38] Though this poem's eagle-eye view of the conflict is provocative (a Palestinian student of mine argued eloquently against the first stanza's dismissive tone toward the *Nakba*), Nye's visionary declaration about the riddle of healing, the possibility of fighting off hate, and the necessity of orienting ourselves toward a future where "everything comes next"[39] is an antidote to the hopeless poisons of past and present.

I can't help returning to Muriel Rukeyser, who always avoided the blood-mongering screeds that some great poets occasionally produced. In her "Poem," we have a chronicle of an ordinary citizen trying to reclaim her own humanity amid the crush of wars and news of wars, punctuated by advertisements.

Poem

I lived in the first century of world wars.
Most mornings I would be more or less insane.
The news would pour out of various devices
The newspapers would arrive with their careless stories,
Interrupted by attempts to sell products to the unseen.
I would call my friends on other devices;
They would be more or less mad for similar reasons.
Slowly I would get to pen and paper,
Make my poems for others unseen and unborn.
In the day I would be reminded of those men and women,
Brave, setting up signals across vast distances,
Considering a nameless way of living, of almost unimagined
    values.
As the lights darkened, as the lights of night brightened,
We would try to imagine them, try to find each other,
To construct peace, to make love, to reconcile
Waking with sleeping, ourselves with each other,
Ourselves with ourselves. We would try by any means
To reach the limits of ourselves, to reach beyond ourselves,
To let go the means, to wake.

I lived in the first century of these wars.[40]

"Poem" anticipates the sort of connectedness only technologi-
cally possible during our own global digital age but with a difference. Rukeyser's requires the intense labor of the imagination
of these others we hope to be reaching, and more than that. To
"reconcile . . . ourselves with each other, / Ourselves with ourselves" in a time of perpetual war. Rukeyser, who hearkens back
to the original meaning of poetry as *poeisis*, a making, once said,
"I will protest all my life. . . . but I'm a person who makes . . .
and I have decided that whenever I protest from now on . . . I
will make something—I will make poems, plant, feed children,
build, but not ever protest without making something. I think
the whole thing must be made again."[41]

Coda

Perhaps peace poetry is not quite a tradition but rather a tendency within poetry and culture. Yet it has been with us as long as we have been writing. Peace poetry—like the peace movement that it anticipates, reflects, and argues with—is part of a larger human conversation about the possibility of a more just and pacific system of social and ecological relations.

The poetry of peace already exists in the footnotes and margins of political and literary history, from Enheduanna to our recent imperial wars in the Middle East. It is a tendency, an itch or irritation, a dormant virus that we've carried with us, a longing like thirst, a half-caught dream, within poetry's longstanding and rocky courtship with power. The poetry of peace is a writing against the grain of received narratives and histories, against the notion that we are doomed to violence and war.

There may come a time when this poetry can be called a tradition. *Come Together: Imagine Peace* was our attempt to draw back in order to move forward, the way a rower leans forward into the water and then digs backward, in order to propel into some new territory. Equally important, *Come Together* offered a bridge between our poetry communities and peace communities, those places where we find ourselves. Poet and Vietnam War veteran W. D. Ehrhart once mused:

> What was the point of my reading antiwar poetry to the members of the Brandywine Peace Community? These are folks who chain themselves to fences and hammer on missile warheads. But what they hear in my poems confirms them in their beliefs (which are not easy to hold and maintain in this culture) . . . and renews their spirit and commitment; it gives them a sense of connectedness, of not being entirely alone. That's worth doing, even if it is on such a small scale (there were maybe 25 people there that night).[42]

Peace poems can be food for the peace troops but also a script for future readings, demonstrations, and other actions. Peace poems, after all, are often occasional endeavors, written by movement participants and delivered for the ear and heart.

Gene Sharp's *Politics of Nonviolent Action* lists 198 nonviolent tactics that resisters have employed to resist illegitimate power and effect social change. Poems can take their place as part of the peace movement story. These poems invite us to join the local networks of the peace movement—which always needs more participants. Poets have a pivotal role to play in the peace movement because of our keen attention to language—not simply to excoriate its abuse by the dominant narrative but also to construct alternative narratives that invite those who may be sympathetic, but lack awareness of the movement, to learn, join, and act.

Peace poems remind us that, though the work of peacemaking is never done, we are not alone, and our voices bear the burden of the silenced throughout the globe. As Rebecca Solnit writes:

> The North American tradition seems to focus its activity on the exposé, the telling of the grim underside of what we know: the food is poison, the system is corrupt, the leaders are lying, the war is failing. There is a place for this, but you cannot base a revolution on the bad things the status quo forgot to mention. You need to tell the stories they are not telling, to learn to see where they are blind, to look at how the great changes of the world come from the shadows and the margins, not center stage, to see where we're winning and that we can win something that matters, if not everything all the time.[43]

The work of peacemaking, and the work of peace poetry, is at least in part to give voice to those small victories—where no blood was spilled, but lives were changed; justice was won; and peace was forged, achieved, or found. And words bring us there, to the brink of something new. Peace poetry is larger than a moral injunction against war; it is an articulation of the expanse, the horizon where we might come together. To adapt a line by the Sufi poet Rumi: *beyond the realm of good and evil, there is a field. / I'll meet you there.*

1. John Keats, "To John Hamilton Reynolds [23]," November 22, 1817, in *Letters of John Keats to His Family and Friends*, ed. Sidney Colvin (London: Macmillan, 1891), 44.

2. John Keats, "To John Hamilton Reynolds [52]," May 3, 1818 (London: Macmillan, 1891), 105.

3. Ezra Pound, "A Few Don'ts by an Imagiste," *Poetry* 1.6 (1913), 201.

4. Denise Levertov, "Making Peace," in *Breathing the Water* (New York: New Directions, 1987), 40.

5. Abraham John Muste, *Gandhi and the H-Bomb: How Nonviolence Can Take the Place of War* (Madison: University of Wisconsin, 1950), quoted in "February 28, A. J. Muste," in *Year with American Saints*, eds. G. Scott Cady and Christopher L. Webber (New York: Church Publishing Inc., 2006), 117.

6. Enheduanna, "Lament to the Spirit of War," trans. Daniela Gioseffi, *Women on War: Essential Voices for the Nuclear Age*, ed. Daniela Gioseffi (Ann Arbor: University of Michigan Press, 1988), 199.

7. Ibid.

8. Dunya Mikhail, "The War Works Hard," in *The War Works Hard* (New York: New Directions, 2005), 6.

9. Archilochus, "On His Shield [29]," *Sappho and the Greek Lyric Poets*, trans. Willis Barnstone (New York: Schocken Books, 1962), 32.

10. Sappho, "Anactoria Poem [16, Lobel-Page]," *The Poetry of Sappho*, trans. Jim Powell (New York: Oxford University Press, 2007), 6.

11. John Milton, "Areopagitica: A Speech of John Milton for the Liberty of Unlicen'd Printing, to the Parlament [sic] of England" (London: British Museum, 1644), 12.

12. Ibid.

13. Michael True, preface to *An Energy Field More Intense Than War: The Nonviolent Tradition and American Literature* (Syracuse: Syracuse University Press, 1995), xi.

14. William Stafford, "Peace Walk," in *Stories That Could Be True: New and Collected Poems* (New York: Harper and Row, 1977), 24.

15. Ibid.

16. Ibid.

17. Robert J. Bertholf, ed., "Notebook 23: November 29, 1957," in "From Robert Duncan's Notebooks: On Denise Levertov," *Jacket* 28 (2005), http://jacketmagazine.com/28/dunc-bert-notebooks.html

18. Levertov, "Making Peace," 40.

19. Ibid.

20. Ibid.

21. Audre Lorde, "Power," *The Black Unicorn* (New York: W. W. Norton, 1978), 108.

22. Ibid., 108–9.

23. Wislawa Szymborska, "The End and the Beginning," trans. Joanna Trzeciak, *Threepenny Review* 70 (1997), https://www.threepennyreview.com/samples/szymborska_su97.html

24. Ibid.

25. Ibid.

26. Yehuda Amichai, "Wildpeace," in *The Selected Poetry of Yehuda Amichai* (Berkeley: University of California Press, 1996), 88.

27. Ibid.

28. Ibid.

29. Ibid., 34.

30. Ibid.

31. Mahmoud Darwish, "A State of Siege," in *The Butterfly's Burden*, trans. Fady Joudah (Port Townsend: Copper Canyon Press, 2007), 129.

32. Ibid., 131–33.

33. Ibid., 153.

34. Ibid., 143.

35. Ibid., 324.

36. Aharon Shabtai, "Lotem Abdel Shafi," trans. Peter Cole, *J'Accuse* (New York: New Directions, 2002), 12.

37. Ibid.

38. Naomi Shihab Nye, "Jerusalem," in *Red Suitcase: Poems* (Rochester: BOA Editions, 1994), 21.

39. Ibid.

40. Muriel Rukeyser, "Poem," in *The Speed of Darkness* (New York: Vintage Books, 1968), 37.

41. Muriel Rukeyser, "Craft Interview with Muriel Rukeyser," *New York Quarterly* 11 (1972): 15–39.

42. W. D. Ehrhart, in discussion with author, July 10, 2005.

43. Rebecca Solnit, "Finding Time," *Orion* 27 (2008): 15.

Erotic Soyuz

25 Propositions on Translating
(Arseny Tarkovsky)

1.

Every essay on (the impossibility of) translation resembles every other, but this one is happy in its own way. Like a striptease that leads only to more clothing, let's begin with a contradiction: generalities are never interesting. The particular is the place of all the juice and joy, all the scald and sin. For example, what's an adequate translation for форточка (*fortochka*)—that little window that opens in a bigger window that does not open?

2.

Another generality masquerading as a particular: language is limestone, porous enough to let the world in and out again, always changed by the water's flow. If poetry is in fact "what is lost in translation," it is because our own words often fail to describe, inscribe, transcribe, or circumscribe our lives. The failures of translation, then, are not failures between languages as much as a property of language itself.

3.

Yet, the translator believes that different languages have enough open edges, even contact zones, like the human body, that they can near or even touch each other. The closer the worlds of those languages (for example, Romance languages or Slavic languages or Finno-Ugric languages), the more edges will fit (almost seamlessly) with other edges. What the translator sees is how many edges have no partner. When I first spent time in Russia, I was amazed how people used the term "на улице" to signify "outside." Literally, the term means "on the street." Another term that Russians use is "на дворе," which means "in the [court]yard." There are many words for outside—снаружи, or exterior—but people don't use it in quite the same way. Inscribed in our languages are slightly different conceptualizations of space. That's why I began the poem "Ashberries," about the time I spent living in Russia: "Outside, in a country with no word for outside, / they cluster on trees, red bunches."[1] Of course this country has a word for outside—it has many words for outside—but what I was gesturing toward was the gap between languages, the gap between different conceptions of space.

4.

Language dictionaries suggest otherwise, but the very fact that words have deep roots makes exact one-to-one word translation difficult, one step more difficult than seeking synonyms in *Roget's Thesaurus*. If you've done this before, you know exactly what I'm talking about. Have a word, then try to find an adequate synonym. Each possibility feels slightly off, like glasses with the wrong prescription. And each synonym for synonym leads you further and further from anything that approximates seeing. Every word, every word worth its salt, carries with it a kind of irreducible particularity—its primal sounds, its weight in the mouth, its richly layered conscious and unconscious connotations and associations, both public and private. Words are like people, only older and more idiosyncratic.

5.

Until the fall of the Soviet Union, there were no words in Russian for "fun," "know-how," "businessman," "discount," "sale," etc. And, of course, the Russians have a whole bag of words associated with Soviet, peasant, and other cultural formations distant from our American experience: How to find a single term for колхоз ("kolkhoz," or "collective farm") or кулак ("kulak," meaning both "landowning peasant" and "fist") that would carry at least some of the connotations of those words? Or, more mundanely, how to find an American English word to describe the acidic reaction one gets from biting into something sour? The Russians have a single word for that: оскомина.

6.

The particular at hand, what we wish to touch, what we wish to touch us, is the work of Russian poet Arseny Tarkovsky, with which I wrestled (in tag-team with Dimitri Psurtsev) for *I Burned at the Feast: Selected Poems of Arseny Tarkovsky* (2015). Tarkovsky, a lifelong poet and translator, the father of the great filmmaker Andrei Tarkovsky, knew himself all too well the miseries of translation, as he wrote in his poem "Translator":

> For what did I spend
> My best years on foreign words?
> O, Eastern translations,
> How you hurt my head.[2]

Actually, of course, he wrote nothing of the kind. He wrote:

> Для чего я лучшие годы
> Продал за чужие слова?
> Ах, восточные переводы,
> Как болит от вас голова.[3]

Or as an email once encoded it:

```
????????????????????????????????
????????????????????????????????
????????????????????????????????
????????????????????????????????
```

Somehow, this seems to be a most adequate representation of the poetics of translation.

7

How can we get close to Tarkovsky? First, there is the fact of Russian poetry's acute and irreducible particularities; the most acute and irreducible being its relationship to meter. The regularity of Russian conjugations and declensions, the flexibility of word order in sentence meaning, and the multisyllabic nature of Russian words all combine to create a seemingly endless wellspring of rhymes and metrical possibilities. In contrast to the poetries of the West, which inhaled modernism's breath of free verse and only rarely return to the formal rooms of strict meters, Russian poetry has, until only very recently, been almost entirely faithful to its highly organized and lush meters. In Tarkovsky's poetry alone, one can find poems not only in iambic but also in dactylic, anapestic, and amphibrachic, not to mention folksongs, unrhymed metrical poems, and, yes, even free verse. It's as if, in the United States, our poetry, metrically speaking, plays its tune within the limits of the pop form, while in Russia, whole symphonies continue to be produced.

8.

But that metaphor suggests a low culture/high culture distinction that distracts from the persistence of complex meters (and rhyme) in Russian poetry. During the twentieth century, when Anglo-American poetry confronted the brave new world of modernism and mass culture, free verse articulated a response to new conditions of production and reception, both to attempt to "make it new" and also resist the new advertising cooptation of the poetic "jingle." In the early Soviet period, poets innovated mightily—from Velemir Khlebnikov's заум (*zaum*) sound poems to Vladimir Mayakovsky's new brutalism in the 1910s and 1920s. But as Socialist Realism began to dominate and many great poets faced repression, the great mnemonic capabilities of Russian poetry served, literally, to allow unpublished poems to persist in the minds of their readers. The story of Nadezhda Mandelstam memorizing her husband Osip's poems, detailed in *Hope against Hope*, is but one stunning example of how Russian poetry's aural commitments (and the Russian people's commitments to poetry) enabled a kind of secret history of the soul to continue: "In order not to forget it, I had to repeat a little to myself each day. . . . There are many women like me who for years have spent sleepless nights repeating the words of their dead husbands over and over."[4]

9.

Even if the Russian literary tradition does delve deep into the darkness and misery and mystery of human existence, the music of Russian poetry is so undeniable, so playful, so often ecstatic, and has persisted for so long, it suggests the secret pleasures of a people who have been seen in the West as the stern patrons of unhappiness ("every unhappy family," etc.). It is, indeed, what makes translating Russian poetry most difficult and why readers of Russian poetry in translation—say, the English poetry version of Anna Akhmatova or Osip Mandelstam—mainly receive a picture of a grim and absurd reality but not much of a sense of what it sounds like when a pure music collides with the grim or the absurd.

10.

Perhaps the translator is a traitor to the native. It's not for nothing that translators are said to use "native informants" to gather intelligence on these strange and dangerous poems. Translators, at times, are literal and figurative colonizers, threatening to domesticate or erase the other in the name of "cultural understanding" or "universal human values." When American translators brought Russian literature into English during the Cold War, it was often summoned to serve a specific political function—not to bring cultural understanding but to bring down the Soviet Union. And when the Soviet Union fell, the government money that had poured into Slavic Departments and presses disappeared overnight.

11.

Of course, what brought me to study Russian poetry may indeed have been Ronald Reagan, who in the 1980s referred to the Soviet Union as the "evil empire." I was immediately intrigued, believing that no people is evil. When I shared this story with poet Sergey Gandlevsky, he said, "you know, when I heard Reagan say that, I thought he was right."[5]

12.

And equally, that the translator can be a traitor to her own people, the way the peacebuilder or a lyric poet can seem a traitor to the tribe. In the words of Charles Simic: "Here is something we can all count on. Sooner or later our tribe always comes to ask us to agree to murder. . . . The lyric poet is almost by definition a traitor to his own people. He is the stranger who speaks the harsh truth that only individual lives are unique and therefore sacred. He may be loved by his people, but his example is also the one to be warned against."[6] The translator lingers in contested territory, where sectarianism compels us/them, ours/theirs. The translator is the one who reminds us that difference is not demonic, but daemonic. The translator, possessed by voices and visions that she can only dimly understand, cannot not speak in this forked (and forked-over) tongue.

13.

Back to Tarkovsky. Tarkovsky's deft and diverse deployment of various meters and rhyme schemes presents an almost insurmountable translation problem: how to demonstrate his near-polyphonic facility for variable patterns of rhythm and sound over the course of many poems, without flattening that work to a dull iambic or free verse style with some half-hearted gesture toward off-rhyme? Dimitri Psurtsev and I considered various, sometimes radical, options. One option, briefly considered: If, in American poetry, the "normative" mode is intonational free verse, then why not make all the "normative" Russian poems with rhyme and meter into that intonational free verse, and all the experimental (free verse or unrhymed poems) into poems with meter and rhyme?

14.

Another, more rigidly systematic option would be simply to translate all the dactylic poems as dactylic poems, the iambics as iambic, and so on. This, frankly, seemed more possible but also literalist, since a poem in dactylic in Russian will mean something different than it will in American poetry. We decided against this rigid and misplaced conservatism, encouraged by the notion of the "semantic aura of meter." Kirill Taranovski (and later Mikhail Gasparov) argues that each meter in Russian poetry carries with it the themes and associations of previous poets' employment of those meters; the very idea that a poem's meters are embedded in a larger discourse of form complicates any simplistic application of meter from poetic tradition to poetic tradition.

15.

Our resolution of this interminable impasse between Russian metric and American poetry has been at once less systematic and more organic. Since Tarkovsky's poetry is driven by its music, propelled by rhythm and rhyme, then our translation should make every reasonable attempt to make a similar music. For example, in his war-era portrait, "Ехал из Брянска в теплушке слепой . . ." ("A blind man was riding"), Tarkovsky employs a dactylic trimeter (plus a final beat) in couplets that echo Nikolay Nekrasov's jaunty folk song meters, creating a dissonant effect with the grim picture of a blind man traveling in the provinces in a cargo train during the Nazi invasion. I began to find the translation in amphibrachs, a peculiar three-part beat of unstressed-stressed-unstressed. The translation begins:

A blind man was riding an unheated train,
From Bryansk he was traveling home with his fate.

Fate whispered to him so the whole car could hear:
And why should you care about blindness and war?

It's good, she was saying, you're sightless and poor.
If you were not blind, you'd never survive . . .[7]

Without rhythm and rhyme, we would risk turning Tarkovsky
into a standard Socialist Realist—losing precisely what makes
him a great Russian poet.

16.

For a free verse poem such as "Град на Первой Мещанской"
("Hail on First Petit-Bourgeois Street"), we opted to remove all
punctuation and create greater disjunction on the level of the
line (even though normative punctuation exists in the original),
in order to reproduce the astonishing effect of free verse to the
Russian ear. Perhaps even this does not quite go as far as recre-
ating the unusual feeling of a Russian reader encountering the
poem:

tongues in the tower
pound the bells to sound
wind lifts   everyone
rushes into entrances   doors
slam   along the sidewalk sandals
patter   rain chasing behind
her heart pounds
her wet dress itches
& the roses are soaked[8]

17.

Translating metrical richness, however, is not the only problem
in translating Tarkovsky. The music of words—from the problem of rhyme to inner alliteration—also presents issues. For example, the war poem "Иванова Ива" (published in *Asymptote*)
relies on the musical play in Russian between "iva" (willow) and
the soldier's name "Ivan."

ИВАНОВА ИВА

Иван до войны проходил у ручья,
Где выросла ива неведомо чья.

Не знали, зачем на ручей налегла,
А это Иванова ива была.

В своей плащ-палатке, убитый в бою,
Иван возвратился под иву свою.

Иванова ива,
Иванова ива,
Как белая лодка, плывет по ручью.[9]

To think: inside the name of the tree is the name of the man. The man inside the tree—as if anticipating the coffin, enclosed inside the wood. Ideally, one might translate this poem as "Will's Willow," which suggests the shared destiny of soldier and the tree of mourning—but such a choice could confuse readers about the place of the poem. We opted for "Valya"—the name of the poet's brother who was killed in the Civil War—which contains the "l" and vaguely echoes the "w" with the "v." Here's our translation, in its entirety:

Valya's Willow

Before the war Valya walked along the creek,
Where a willow grew for who knows who.

Though why it lay on the creek, no one knew
Valya owned that willow.

Killed in action, Valya came back
Under his willow, in his military cloak.

Valya's willow,
Valya's willow,
Like a white boat floating on the creek.[10]

18

Finally, there is the problem of translating Tarkovsky's own world—both his cultural-historical context and his own personal vision. In "К Стихам" ("To Poems"), Tarkovsky's characteristic quasi-Christian pantheism explores the origins of his poetry, addressing his own poems as if they were his children. It ends:

I had long been the earth—
Arid, ochre, forlorn since birth—
But you fell on my chest by chance
From beaks of birds, from eyes of grass.[11]

These final lines presented a confusion that thankfully was clarified by the late poet and translator F. D. Reeve, who noted that the "eyes of grass" is a reference to how fields of grasses would contain wildflowers, whose "eyes" would seed the earth. In what is an all too typical problem in translation, what appeared to be pure abyssal surrealism—"eyes of grass"—was an associative leap from one place to another place, very much on (and in!) earth. How stunning that a poet of such great humility (from *humus*, earth) is able to pull off speaking as earth.

19.

Or this poem, "Бабочка в госпитальном саду" ("Butterfly in the Hospital Orchard"), about Tarkovsky's days on the edge between life and death after his gangrenous leg required multiple amputations. The lightness and beauty of the meter and rhyme, as if following the motions of the butterfly, hovers just outside all catching it. The word play at the end of the second stanza of the poem relates to the fact that the word for butterfly, "бабочка," has only two vowels—"a" and "o." It's as if this creature, at its center, produces only the vowels of awe: A! O! The English vowels "u" and "y" became a matrix of existential questioning, and while I like it, it lacks the utter wonder of the Russian.

Butterfly in the Hospital Orchard

Flying from shadow into the light,
She is herself both shadow and light.

Where did she come from, this being
Nearly naked of markings?
She hops in the air when she's flying.
She must be from Asia
There's no one quite like her here.
She must be from forgotten years,
Where the smallest drop of azure
Is like a blue sea in our eyes.

She swears it will be "forever"
But keeps the word "never."
She can hardly count to two,
Understands less than little,
And from the whole alphabet knows
Only a few vowels—

> U
> &
> Y.

The butterfly's name is a picture
Impossible to pronounce. And why
Does she have to be so quiet?
She's like a simple mirror.

Don't fly off to the East, O
My lady! Don't chase the East,
Flying from shadows
Into the light. My soul, why
Do you long for a far-off place?
O my colorful beloved, my lady,
Don't fly away.[12]

20.

It turns out that failure—the dominant metaphor in so much
talk about translation—is not the right metaphor at all. How's
this? Translation is erotic/asymptotic—about nearing, longing,
stretching one's language toward what it might become. The
original as sacred text toward which we long. If poetry is, as Allen Grossman has proposed, an Orphic attempt to reach the

Beloved, then the translator is nothing if not Orpheus, at every moment longing to turn and be sure that the beloved still follows. Only a complete turn back will cause the beloved to fade forever. I'm reminded, suddenly, of the moment I learned that in written Russian, "you" is always capitalized, and "I" is not.

21.

Or this: translation as transformation. Translation as a co-creative, procreative act. Two languages come together and make a third thing. Robert Lowell's notorious *Imitations*, treat the original texts not as an impossibly distant object of idealization but a source of inspiration and invitation, something to meet and make love with. Fady Joudah recently said that he wished his translations of Palestinian poet Mahmoud Darwish were not in English, but "Arabish." May these Tarkovsky poems be "Russianish."

22.

Translations are beautiful monsters. If all translators are Frankenstein, the main question then becomes: Is the creature alive? Those grab bags of other organs and skin, stolen from the graveyards of other traditions whose sensibilities are not always our own, grafted into something that approximates a whole. Has the translator provided the lightning rod, gathered the electricity? Monstrous beauty, do you breathe?

23.

Since the 1960s, the Russians have flown a series of spacecraft called Союз. Soyuz. We have heard it pronounced "Soy-use," emphasis on the "soy." *I am*, but only in Spanish. In Russian, it sounds like "sigh-use," the emphasis on "use." It means "union." To think: all these Unions flying about the sky, hovering above and around our planet, into space.

24.

These Unions, in fact, have something called *translation thrusters*. Translation, in physics, describes the "motion of a body in which every point of the body moves parallel to and the same distance as every other point of the [other] body."[13]

25.

In the end, translators believe in the possibility of translation, as poets must believe in the impossibility of translation—even as they engage in that impossible process with every poem, even in their native tongue. But difference does not lead, necessarily, to irreconcilability. So this: that the two language-poems work on their relation, to find those points parallel, the edges that hold against other edges—providing a fit that each will wear, and will wear each, in its own way.

Notes

1. Philip Metres, "Ashberries: Letters," *To See the Earth* (Cleveland, OH: Cleveland State Poetry Center, 2008), 11.

2. Philip Metres, unpublished translation.

3. Arseny Tarkovsky, "Translator," *Sobranie Sochenenii. Tom Pervyi* (Moscow: Khodozhestvennaya Literatura, 1991), 92.

4. Nadezhda Mandelstam, *Hope Against Hope*, trans. Max Hayward (New York: Atheneum, 1970), 276.

5. Sergey Gandlevsky, in discussion with author.

6. Charles Simic, *The Unemployed Fortune-Teller* (Ann Arbor: University of Michigan Press, 1994), 37–38.

7. Arseny Tarkovsky, *I Burned at the Feast: Selected Poems*, trans. Philip Metres and Dimitri Psurtsev (Cleveland, OH: Cleveland State University Press, 2015), 43.

8. Ibid., 9.

9. Ibid., 52.

10. Ibid., 53.

11. Ibid., 101.

12. Ibid., 51.

13. *The American Heritage Science Dictionary* (New York: Houghton Mifflin, 2005), 638.

Homing In

The Place of Poetry in the Global Digital Age

My wife and I went shopping for smart phones recently, beholding these modern votives with equal parts wonder and worry. We, digital immigrants and introverts who tote a decade-old "flip" phone only for emergencies, see the benefits of these magical devices. They have the fairy-tale power of a digital genie, released with the mere swipe of a screen. But what genie will we unleash when we bring this technology into our lives? Doesn't the servant, in the end, always change the master?

Despite the fact that digital technologies offer global connectedness, they also appear to isolate us further into our own self-created reality, dislocate us from the non-digital world. And the greater our privilege, the more we can cordon off the real, the stronger our myopia. Amiri Baraka once wrote: "Luxury, then, is a way of / being ignorant, comfortably."[1] Yet privilege does more than damage our vision; it starves the heart. In the Biblical parable of Lazarus and the Rich Man, the rich man's flaw is not merely being unable to see Lazarus in pain right outside his gate; after his death, when the rich man looks up from Hades, he clearly recognizes Lazarus next to Abraham in heaven, and begs Abraham to ask Lazarus for a bit of water to cool his torment. The rich man knows Lazarus by name, but even in hell, does not see fit to address him directly.

In our global digital age—with its information flood, its attenuation of attention, its transmogrification of subjectivity, its obscuring of our connectedness—what can poetry and the arts do? The artist's challenge is not merely to chronicle the hectic present but to develop an understanding of how we find ourselves at this time and place, to explore what binds us to each other, and to address the question: "How then shall we live?"

179

Poetry's oldest and least-marketable power, paradoxically, offers us a secret vitality. Poetry's slowness, its ruminativity, enables us to step back from the distracted and distracting present, to ground ourselves again through language in the realities of our bodies and spirits and their connections to the ecosystems in which we find ourselves. The form of a poem is one that forms us, holding us in its thrall. To dwell with singular lines or phrases, lines that puzzle or clarify, carries us back to the ancient practices of ritual chant and shamanic trance, fundamental to the ecstatic possibilities of communion and healing. In the words of C. D. Wright, *pace* Horace: "Some of us do not read or write particularly for pleasure or instruction, but to be changed, healed, charged."[2]

Poetry, at its root, is a "making" (*poesis*). This making is often akin to prayer, or parallel to prayer—a reaching for or an appeal to the great mystery of the Beloved, the Great Maker. One of the things I love about Ignatian spirituality is its fundamental emphasis on an active imagination, what St. Ignatius calls "*composición*"—often translated as "seeing in imagination" or "mental representation."[3] *Composición* comes from the Latin *compositionem*, meaning "putting together, connecting," but the word's roots suggest that imaginative visualization involves placing oneself with ("com" plus "position"). The imagination can locate us in our own lives (what Ignatius calls the Daily Examen), as well as bring us to far-flung places, to stand with others. Ignatius asks the Exercitant, for example, in contemplating the Nativity, to "see . . . in imagination the way from Nazareth to Bethlehem. Consider its length, its breadth; whether level, or through valleys and over hills. Observe the place where Christ is born; whether big or little; whether high or low; and how it is arranged."[4] Such grounded visionary practice is both exercise and meditation. The work of the imagination invites us to slow down, pay close attention, to visualize, to wonder. Poetry tunes us to ultimate things.

Poetry is not a mere throwback, some atavistic practice for the vestigial few. On the contrary, poetry's discipline of entering us into our minds and bodies—our restless bodies, our roiled souls—is an ancient practice that invites grace to enter our brokenness, to hold us together, to waken us again. The

Sufi poet Rumi wrote, the wound is the place "where the light enters you,"[5] seven hundred years before Leonard Cohen sang, "There's a crack in everything. That's how the light gets in"[6]— thus proving Thomas Merton's thesis that "that which is oldest is . . . most new."[7]

Poetry is also a technology of embodied inquiry, a way of locating ourselves and others within contexts heretofore outside of our understanding, yet which include us within their operations. Michael Davidson has proposed that "perhaps poetry, in its proximity to affective states, is the dreamwork of globalization."[8] Poetry and the arts indeed can help us perform what Fredric Jameson calls cognitive mapping, "enabl[ing] a situational representation on the part of the individual subject to that vaster and properly unrepresentable totality which is the ensemble of society's structures as a whole."[9] I love this strange quote; Jameson, a postmodern Marxist theorist, has in mind a materialist totality and that we are subjects (and objects) in the system of late capitalism. Yet, Jameson's phrasing is mystical, inviting us to consider not only human structures but also planetary, cosmic structures. Perhaps, even, the unrepresentable Divine.

Cosmopoetics is a good way to describe art that performs cognitive mapping. It suggests both cosmopolitanism—the philosophy of global human solidarity—and also something cosmic, where the universe offer us traces of a great Totality. When I look at my own writing—which began only as a blind reaching-out into the epistemological dark—a cosmopoetics, a geographical imagination, seems to have taken shape. Like many poets, I began writing to make sense of what was happening to me and around me; as my interests have orbited further outward, I was challenged—and the language challenged me—to reach beyond comfortable frames of understanding. Each place became a portal to new worlds. Traveling to my grandparents' houses in Brooklyn or Rhode Island, or climbing inside the ancient step pyramid at Chichén Itzá, or after college, living in Russia for a year, were quantum leaps where my language flailed to reach for some sort of handhold.

The questions of travel, as Elizabeth Bishop called them, have often been at the center of my writing. Travel exposes us to otherness (other cultures, other histories, other people), and exposes us as other to ourselves. Yet, as Mary Louise Pratt argues in *Imperial Eyes*, the trope of "anti-conquest" in Western travel writing—in which an innocent Westerner encounters other places and culture—becomes a strategy of representation that enables one to "seek to secure their innocence at the same moment as they assert European hegemony."[10] So many writers have exploited their travel experience as yet another subject to plunder, the imagination as a marauding imperial Columbus. That's why in one poem, in *To See the Earth*, I cite my Russian mentor, Dimitri Psurtsev, who once remarked after reading some of my poems, "this is your version of Russia, not Russia."

When I speak of "cognitive mapping," of cosmopoetics, I am talking about an essential human endeavor—to connect our apperceptive physicality to our surroundings. It's a dirty little secret, but I love getting lost, because getting lost also entails a new kind of knowing. Just when you think you know where you're going, you're lost. When you see you're lost, you're going to find something larger than the self.

Yet cartography and its abstractions are deeply political and often have extended exploitative power arrangements, which carved people and peoples apart for the aims of empires. That's why I'm wary of broad claims about the representativity of my representations. *To See the Earth* is "my" creation story, *Pictures at an Exhibition* is "my" Russia, *A Concordance of Leaves* is "my" Palestine, and *Sand Opera* is "my" Iraq. Or rather, this is where "I" come from, this is the Russia in which I lost and found myself, the Palestine that absorbed me, the Iraq that carries me.

Sand Opera began as a daily Lenten meditation, working with the testimonies of the tortured at Abu Ghraib, to witness to their suffering; it became an attempt to find a language that would sight (to render visible) and site (to locate in the geographical imagination) the war itself, constantly off-screen. War is so distanced that the closest most Americans get to it is when they encounter a veteran or refugee. That it was illegal for eighteen years—from 1991's Operation Desert Storm until 2009—to take photos of flag-draped coffins of U.S. military suggests the level of censorship during war. This policy is designed not only to abstract the enemy but also to render the cost of war invisible and suppress domestic questioning. More recently, the program of "targeted assassination" by drones has yet to be made fully apparent to the American people.

My desire in *Sand Opera* is to make the Iraq War and the wider War on Terror visible, to make a visible and audible map of it, a map that we would carry in our eyes and ears, in our bodies and hearts, to replace the maps of pundits and demagogues. As a poet, I wanted to do this mostly through language—often through language that renders the ruptures of violence, through the black bars of redaction and fractured syntax—but I also found myself drawn to the strange images that point toward the operations of war.

Throughout the book, for example, unexplained drawings of rooms appear, with language floating on a vellum page above them. These are renderings by Mohamad Bashmilah, a former prisoner from Yemen, of what have come to be known as *black sites*—secret prisons where the United States and its allies would illegally interrogate detainees. These drawings are the renderings of one who has been "rendered," sundered from everything he knew. To witness them is to enter the mind of a person utterly dislocated, yet rigorously, obsessively, trying to locate himself.

Sand Opera also contains a diagram of a proper "Muslim Burial" from the Standard Operation Procedure manual for the Guantanamo Bay prison. The SOP notes the importance of the treatment of the body—the enshrouding process, the prayers that should be uttered—and how the body should point toward Mecca. Alongside the testimonies of prisoners who saw the Qu'ran thrown into the toilet, we are struck again by the gap between our measure of cultural sensitivity and our manipulation of that knowledge for cruel and degrading acts.

A poem is a momentary home, a way to home in. Their architectures, their forms, inform how we perceive and feel insides and outsides. In *Sand Opera*, we stumble among the broken syntax of the tortured in the Abu Ghraib prison; we stare at the thick walls of the vellum-paged "Black Site (Exhibit I)," trying to read the words on the next page seeping around the prison cell. We confront the words of a bereaved widow of a soldier who has the chance to enter the military tank where her husband died, in "Home Sweet Home," nested inside another poem, based on a letter of a Marine lamenting his own entrapment in a war where he can't fight the evil he faces. War always comes home, not just in the bodies and minds of military veterans but also in the militarization of prisons and police; the distance between Ferguson and Baghdad is closer than some would like to think.

Cosmopoetics is ultimately not just about mapping, or even seeing. It's also about listening, about a radical vulnerability to the other. As Isaiah writes, "morning after morning / He opens my ear that I may hear."[11] *Sand Opera* is the sound of my listening. These poems carry forth voices that have opened me—the Iraqi curator Donny George Youkhanna, sharing slides of lost art from his cherished museum, abused Iraqi prisoners and U.S. military at the Abu Ghraib prison, a recipe in Nawal Nasrallah's Iraqi cookbook, the detained Mohamad Bashmilah, a drone operator who isn't sure who he's killing, an Arab-American living through the paranoid days after the 9/11 attacks, and my daughter's coming to consciousness in a world where war leaks through the radio and television. The words of my daughter at the end of the poem "Hung Lyres" embody what I hope I can continue to open myself into.

From "Hung Lyres"

What does it mean, I say. She says, it means
to be quiet, just by yourself. She says, there's

a treasure chest inside. You get to dig it out.
Somehow, it's spring. Says, will it always

rain? In some countries, I say, they are
praying for rain. She asks, why do birds sing?

In the dream, my notebook dipped in water,
all the writing lost. Says, read the story again.

But which one? That which diverts the mind
is poetry. Says, you know those planes

that hit those buildings? Asks, why do birds sing?
When the storm ends, she stops, holds her hands

together, closes her eyes. What are you doing?
I'm praying for the dead worms. Says, listen:[12]

How can we map these connections and distances without losing our focus on what's directly in front of us—this tendency
toward *hyperopia*, that long sightedness that is another kind of
myopia? I've thought a lot about all the ways that my obsessions
with distant wars and places and people have frayed me to loose
ends, distracting me from intimate joys and domestic peace. At
times, I've wondered if I've engaged in the poetic equivalent
of the father scrolling through his phone while his child finally
balances on her bike and glides down the sidewalk, in perfect
rhythm with herself and her conveyance. How to hold the sight
of my daughters' faces, dearer to me than any faces on this dear
earth, alongside the sight of someone else's daughter's face—
first seen on Facebook—pulling schoolbooks out of a bombed
house in Gaza, to continue studying another day? How to hold
and be held by my beloved wife, and also teach my classes, catch
up on emails and messages, mow the lawn, take out the garbage,
and also find time to click a microloan to a Gazan farmer named
Ahmad, who needs to buy some hens for his egg business? How
do we carry our others and ourselves on this fragile planet?

Antonio Gramsci once asked himself so poignantly: "[is] it
really possible to forge links with a mass of people when one has
never had strong feelings for anyone, not even one's own parents, if it is possible to have a collectivity when one has not been
deeply loved oneself by individual human creatures. Hasn't
[this] . . . tended to make me sterile and reduce my quality as a
revolutionary by making everything a matter of pure intellect, of
pure mathematical calculation?"[13] Gramsci's question is an old
theme, as old as Diogenes' idea of cosmopolitanism. The cosmopolitan idea that we are all connected and that a person on a
distant part of the globe is as dear as our neighbor has always en-
gendered the profoundest critique of the cosmopolite—that he
is one who loves everyone in the abstract but hates (or ignores)
all particular people. It's a real danger I have occasionally blun-
dered into, blinkered by vanity or distracted by novelty.

Poetry is one of the ways we might try to home in—to claim
our own ground—not our digital platforms but the raw earthi-

185

ness of our own bodies, our beloveds, our kin, our distant next-door (human and sentient) neighbors of the communities in which we live and ones to which we're tied. Like any other technology, poetry contains powers that both distract and focus us; it is a danger like any power. Yet it is one of the ways I answer the question—how to ground myself in my own body, my breath, exercising something I have no other word for but *love*, that radical opening of self to the other? "For we are put on this earth a little space," William Blake writes, "that we may learn to bear the beams of love."[14]

I'd like to circle back to the smart phone for a moment. It's strange to think that the very smart phone that enables you to Google Map your way in any strange city in the world doesn't advertise that the rare earths that go into its construction (exotic elements such as tantalum, tungsten, tin, and gold) may have come from—and fueled conflict in—places such as the Congo. And once a new model emerges and we've worn out the phone, where does this material go when we've thrown it out? Whose child will be paid pennies to pull out its innards? Who will inherit its poisons?

I trace my awakening to this question from my early days at Loyola Academy, where, in a freshman religious studies class taught by the improbably ancient Father Steenken, we watched "The Wrath of Grapes"—a documentary exposé on pesticide exposure to migrant workers—and the filmic adaptation of Ambrose Bierce's "Occurrence at Owl Creek Bridge." Ignatian spirituality—from social justice conscientization to existential exploration of a condemned man's longing for freedom—lit my imagination and dilated my empathy. What I long to write and to encounter is art that can help us make a quantum leap in our moral imagination. As a poet, I long for Isaiah's fire, for a "well-trained tongue, / That I might know how to speak to the weary / A word that will rouse them."[15] To make poems that will open not only our eyes but awaken us, pry open our hearts and souls, induce μετάνοια (*metanoia*)—transforming how we spend our breath on this earth.

I'd like to end with a poem that is also a prayer.

Compline

That we await a blessed hope, & that we will be struck
With great fear, like a baby taken into the night, that every
    boot,

Every improvised explosive, Talon & Hornet, Molotov
& rubber-coated bullet, every unexploded cluster bomblet,

Every Kevlar & suicide vest & unpiloted drone raining fire
On wedding parties will be burned as fuel in the dark
    season.

That we will learn the awful hunger of God, the nerve-
    fraying
Cry of God, the curdy vomit of God, the soiled swaddle of
    God,

The constant wakefulness of God, alongside the sweet scalp
Of God, the contented murmur of God, the limb-twitched
    dream-

Reaching of God. We're dizzy in every departure, limb-lost.
We cannot sleep in the wake of God, & God will not sleep

The infant dream for long. We lift the blinds, look out into
    ink
For light. My God, my God, open the spine binding our
    sight.[16]

Notes

1. Amiri Baraka, "Political Poem," *The Le-Roi Jones/Amiri Baraka Reader* (New York: Basic Books, 2000), 73.

2. C. D. Wright, *Cooling Time: An American Vigil* (Port Townsend, WA: Copper Canyon, 2012), 55.

3. Louis J. Puhl, S. J., ed., *The Spiritual Exercise of St. Ignatius* (Chicago: Loyola University Press, 1951), 170.

4. Ibid., 52.

5. Rumi, *The Essential Rumi*, ed. Coleman Barks (San Francisco, CA: HarperSanFrancisco, 1995), 141.

6. Leonard Cohen, "Anthem," 1992.

7. Thomas Merton, *New Seeds of Contemplation* (New York: New Directions Press, 2007), 107.

8. Michael Davidson, *On the Outskirts of Form: Practicing Social Poetics* (Middletown: Wesleyan University Press, 2011), 50.

9. Fredric Jameson, *Postmodernism: Or, the Cultural Logic of Late Capitalism* (Durham, NC: Duke University Press, 1991), 51.

10. Mary Louise Pratt, *Imperial Eyes: Travel Writing and Transculturation* (New York: Routledge, 1992), 7.

11. Isaiah 50:4 (NABRE).

12. Philip Metres, *Sand Opera* (Farmington, ME: Alice James Books, 2015), 56.

13. Qtd. in Giuseppe Fiori, *Antonio Gramsci: Life of a Revolutionary* (New York: Dutton, 1971), 157)

14. William Blake, "The Little Black Boy," in *Selected Poems of William Blake* (New Hampshire: Heinemann, 1996), 9.

15. Isaiah, op. cit., online.

16. Metres, op. cit., 97.

By Heart

On Memorizing Poems

It was one of those gray days, made grayer by the tinted windows of Chicago's O'Hare airport, "the busiest airport in the world" living up to its name. People swirled in a hectic river past me as I slouched, awaiting my connecting flight to return home to Cleveland. A man about thirty years old sat down across the way, lurking furtively toward me.

"Excuse me," he said, "did you teach English at John Carroll?"

"Still do. Weren't you one of my students?" He looked vaguely familiar, though thicker in his body than the lanky, quiet boy ten years before who had sat toward the back of class in Major American Writers.

He was an actuary now, which he explained has something to do with statistics and predicting the future, but all he wanted to do was talk about the past.

"I still remember the poem," he said, and leaned in.

In the middle of the hurtle of human beings heading to their gates, heading home, he spoke:

> Whose woods these are I think I know.
> His house is in the village though;
> He will not see me stopping here
> To watch his woods fill up with snow. . . .[1]

For many of my courses, I require students to memorize a poem, which they recite or write down in class, before they write a paper about it.

It is a weird, annoying, old-fashioned assignment, which is secretly ancient, crazy, and beautiful: to hold and share words by heart. To use your mouth, your whole body, as an instrument for the unfettered music of words.

It's a nearly forgotten art, having things by heart. Alongside discus, wrestling, and running, the ancient Greek Olympics featured competitive poetry recitation. Though it's now considered suspicious and undemocratic, rote learning of all sorts was a dominant mode through much of human history. Even in the nineteenth and early twentieth centuries, Anglo-American culture featured numerous reciters of Bible verses, ready to delight and instruct parlor parties and church halls, for the greater edification of both performer and audience. Once a staple of education, recitation in the West has fallen almost entirely out of favor, as both poetry and memorization have been downgraded as useless modalities for the digital age; mostly, memorization is a cramming exercise for pre-med students learning anatomy or history students and their dates to wars they'll quickly off-load once they've finished the exam. Memory itself is now so supplemented by digitization, it seems nearly impossible to have actual memories that aren't computer-generated.

Some modern poets have argued that memorization can distract us from the poem, failing to exist in mindful relation to it; Ron Silliman notably worried that "to recite a poem, one is required to have the whole of it in mind, to be ever vigilant as to one's position—the way an actor has to be on stage—with all of its past and its future right at the surface of awareness. One is perpetually other than present with the text at hand."[2] He's not entirely wrong; reciting a poem requires a decidedly different relationship to a poem than sitting with a poem and reading it.

But as long as our species has been speaking, we've held some lines of language by heart. A prayer that consoles: *make me an instrument of your peace.* A commercial jingle. A dirty joke. Something about a girl from Nantucket. The pledge of allegiance. Something a parent or a friend or a teacher said that we've never forgotten, that bore a hole into us, hurting or healing. Whole pop songs or church hymns sometimes well up, when its melody opens and lights something inside us. All of us carrying these words that carry us.

Actors, singers, politicians, rappers, motivational speakers, the religious—by our trade, some of us make a living reciting, the medium and message all mixed into one. In the words of Dan Beachy-Quick, "Memorizing a poem, in a strange sort of way, gives that poem access to you more than you're giving yourself access to it. . . . It's as if it creates a new channel of intelligence in me that isn't mine at all."[3]

During Stalin's rule, when the Russian poet Osip Mandelstam was hauled off to die in a Siberian gulag because he'd written an unflattering poem about the leader, Nadezhda Mandelstam secured her husband's memory—his patrimony of poetry—by memorizing, one by one, hundreds of his poems. Her mind was a cathedral she'd made of thousands and thousands of words.

When the mayor of Belfast—who was hosting our peacebuilding immersion group—learned I was a poet, he asked if I could recite one of my poems for him. Because what sort of poet did not carry words with him, closer than his clothes? After all, that is the Irish bardic way. I offered him a short poem, hoping it was adequate to the occasion. I wondered whether it would have been better to pull out some lines from Yeats or Heaney, like

History says, Don't hope
On this side of the grave,
But then, once in a lifetime
The longed-for tidal wave
Of justice can rise up
And hope and history rhyme.[4]

One fall, I went on a two-week tour with the Russian poet Sergey Gandlevsky, who would recite all of his poems by heart. I would doggedly read the translations, and he would stand, look off into the distance, and in his bass of a voice call forth these whole word-worlds that he had made. By heart. To this day, his two-hour-long readings are hypnotic events, performances of a life's work. Each time I am with him, it reminds me that poetry is much more than a stretch of verse, words knocked together in some pleasing way, but an alternate way of being. He'd later tell me that he didn't memorize his poems. No, he'd written them, line by line, in his head. That's how they were composed, not on the page, but as he walked, speaking them to himself over days and weeks and even months.

It hearkens back to the days when masses of people—all over the world—carried words with them that reminded them of where they came from, where they were, and where they were going. Stitched deep in us, there is this need to remember, to pass on.

Elsewhere, this practice still lives. Legendary recitations of the Qu'ran, the Mahabharata, and all manner of great religious and epic verses now span the globe, flying through digital networks from server to server. On YouTube, I just watched Yaseen Rajab, a Syrian boy, imitate the recitation styles of famous qāri's, on a television show a la "The Voice," for a panel of judges who can find only praise and thanks for the boy and his dulcet voice.

But some recitation remains outside the virtual world, embodied by the singer and anchored to the land which it maps. Aboriginal Australians retain the tradition of navigating the land through songlines, also called "dreamtracks." The songs themselves are a kind of poetic global positioning system, whereby the song anchors the singer in the landscape and helps them figure out where they need to go. Likewise, in *Country of My Skull*, South African writer Antije Krog recalls a meeting with poets from Senegal and Morocco, who share what it means to be a poet. For the Berber poet, poetry is no language game; for this nomadic people, poetry is a mnemonic of survival, anchored in place, to survive life in the arid climes of the Sahara:

> In my culture, the task of the poet is to remember the watering places—the metrical feet of the water holes. The survival of the whole group depends on whether you can find the water holes in the desert. You must remember them in such a way that other groups are none the wiser. The group will never cast you out or see you as mad—but the day you betray the position of the water holes to someone else, that is the day they will leave the poet behind in the dunes.[5]

Krog means for us to think of this definition metaphorically. That sometimes the poem is a secret only for the tribe—to remember the watering places for its own survival; and the consequences of sharing that secret can be dangerous, because if everyone knows the places of the watering holes, then they will be used up. The implication is that some poems are not for everyone. But those for whom these poems exist—they will be kept alive by them.

Too often I wish poetry had a wider and more significant presence in our cultural life; it seems that we need poetry, and its ruminative mysteries, more than ever. I thirst for its quiet and its questions, its enigmas and its wonder, and worry that that we have lost something immeasurable in the process of losing it and its watering places.

Sometimes I need a poem or a prayer—a mouthful of words, a mantra—just to fall asleep, when my heart or head suddenly races in the stillness of late-night. Back in O'Hare airport, surrounded by the seethe of people carrying their own languages and their own silences, when this old student stumbled on a line, I picked it up, and then we finished the poem together:

> The woods are lovely, dark and deep,
> But I have promises to keep.
> And miles to go before I sleep,
>
> And miles to go before I sleep.[6]

Notes

1. Robert Frost, "Stopping By Woods on a Snowy Evening," *Selected Poems* (New York: Holt, Rinehart, and Winston, Inc., 1963), 140.

2. Ron Silliman, *Silliman's Blog.* May 4, 2005. http://ronsilliman.blogspot.com/2005/05/whenever-ive-been-paired-up-at-reading.html

3. Dan Beachy-Quick, "Inscribe the Poem on Yourself," interviewed by Curtis Fox. *Poetry off the Shelf,* podcast audio. December 12, 2011. Accessed January 26, 2017. https://www.poetryfoundation.org/features/audio/detail/76106

4. Seamus Heaney, "Voices from Lemnos," *Opened Ground: Selected Poems 1966–1996* (New York: Farrar, Straus, & Giroux, 1998), 305–6.

5. Antjie Krog, *Country of My Skull: Guilt, Sorrow, and the Limits of Forgiveness in the New South Africa* (New York: Crown, 2007), 292.

6. Robert Frost, op. cit., 140.

Dialogue III

Parsing Arias

A Dialogue through "abu ghraib arias" with Micah Cavaleri

The following is a condensed version of an email correspondence between Iraq War veteran and poet Micah Cavaleri and Philip Metres that took place between June and September, 2011.

MICAH CAVALERI: The religious fragments of your book transform an account of torture into a sort of theodicy, like the book of Job. An attempt to confront or transform evil. Although evil may be too big and airy a notion. Disgusting, maybe, is the word. In "The Blues of Charles Graner," there is the explicit acknowledgment of the disagreement between Graner's Christian values and what he values in his role as a corrections officer: "can't / help but love / making a grown man / piss himself."[1]

The (echo /ex /) sections combine ancient religious/ moral texts with accounts of torture at Abu Ghraib, which, initially, draw attention to the conflict Graner noted by the difference on the page between the style of the notes on torture, sometimes faded, sometimes an ordinary black type, while the ancient texts are set in darker lettering or italicized. Strangely, though, the ancient texts intermingle with the Abu Ghraib accounts to produce beautiful, musical pieces, where I am drawn away from the conflict of values and wonder at what is being said about notions of holiness and scripture. For instance, the character of G functions as both Graner the torturer and God the creator and torturer:

G came and laughed

lo, in her mouth

it will break again

arms behind

broken because I can't

sever pain[2]

Again, there is this perfect instance of the melding of the role of torturer and creator/life-giver:

In the beginning   I was there for 67 days

of

██████████   torture I saw myself *on*

the face

of the deep   *And the darkness he called Night*

And Graner released

my hand from the door and he cuffed my hand in the back. [3]

The confusion of torturer and creator challenges the place of religion as anything like a moral guide, at the same time it places religious values next to roles Americans (claim to) value, in this case, the role of a soldier at war, undermining the claim to be able to hold both . . . what . . . religious values and patriotic/American values? What is most interesting to me, though, at least right now, is the way that you're weaving together of what we consider such radically different texts leads to a reading that finds holiness in an act of torture. In the second quote, for example, "67 days of / [torture]" resolves itself with the victim falling into some sort of mystical vision where he says "I saw myself *on the face / of the deep And the darkness he called Night* / And Graner released / my hand from the door."[4]

PHILIP METRES: You capture something exactly when you call the arias a theodicy, my poetic witness to and struggle with the question of—for lack of a better term—evil, and whether one might believe in a God that would allow such suffering. The arias emerged from long meditation on the Abu Ghraib prison scandal, in which I decided that I could not write my way into those photographs of abuse taken by the military police at Abu Ghraib. Only when I stumbled on transcripts of the testimony given by the Iraqi prisoners themselves did I discover a way to slip inside that prison.

And yes, the Charles Graner poem highlights the contradictions at the heart of each of us who professes to be Christian and yet finds ourselves acting against the primal love of Jesus. Nowhere is the contradiction of Christian life as extreme as in war—yet ironically, many American soldiers profess to being deeply religious, even devout. Reading the transcripts of Iraqis abused at Abu Ghraib, one feels as if we are reading a perverse version of Genesis, in which God is a de-creator. Graner, perhaps, as Obscene Father.

You've put your finger on what is perhaps the most unsettling aspect of writing this poem and perhaps writing any poetry that witnesses to violence; are we making such violence beautiful, and therefore somehow missing its profoundly traumatic core? Are we aestheticizing other people's pain? I hope not, but it's not for me to say. Robert Hass' poem "Winged and Acid Dark" has become for me a guide for how one can write affirmatively and humbly about the difficulty of navigating the horror and beauty that exists simultaneously, always, often in the same spaces and times. Some poets fetishize horror, and some poets pretend the knowable world is the circumference of grass just outside their studio window. All I know is that I cannot not look away. But the horror of the world is not the (only) truth of the world.

I'm writing to you from Belfast, Northern Ireland, and have been leading a group of students and faculty in a course on peacebuilding. For a number of the people that we have met, the moment of *metanoia* was when they recognized in the pain of the other their own pain, when they saw how they were suffering together. Bill Shaw, a Protestant who grew up in the Loyalist enclave of Sandy Row, said he was 17 before he met a

Catholic. When Bill met Sean, a Catholic, at their workplace, Bill began to see Catholics as human beings, that the two of them just wanted to have a pint together and meet girls. Yet every night, after their pint, they each took the bus back to their separate neighborhoods. How long it took for them to be able to reach outside of their enclaves, their boxes, and forge a friendship that would overcome those barriers, both internal and external.

The work of grassroots peacebuilding is fundamentally about relationship, and the situation of war constantly ossifies our identities as national beings. You know better than I how being a soldier narrows the possibilities of human being, human relation, despite the amazing opportunities that one may have with working with fellow soldiers and local people. I'd be curious to hear how you respond to this poem as a soldier, in particular, if that is not too difficult!

MC: In America, we celebrate soldiers. In the army, General Lee is nearly a god . . . or at least a saint. And the movie *The Last Samurai* idealizes the samurai as grounded in Buddhism. But what are soldiers in reality, and what is war? No one seems to want to really answer those questions. Our answers are usually something like the movie *Blackhawk Down*, a wonderful movie that skips over guys going home and beating their wives or killing themselves. *The Last Samurai* ignores the thuggish nature of the samurai as a mercenary. And General Lee . . . well, he said it best: True patriotism sometimes requires of men to act exactly contrary, at one period, to that which it does at another.[5] Or, more gently, war and soldiering is: "Something not sayable /spurting from the morning silence, / secret as a thrush."[6]

War is disgusting. The people involved in it are often disgusting. (You see I avoid the word evil.) War and politics (and scripture/holiness) transform everything unrecognizably. I mean, we want to justify our wars, call them moral, but I am not sure how morality applies. War is a sublime, formless object.

PM: When the arias found their other half—that is, the words of the Standard Operating Procedure and of U.S. soldiers—I knew that it was almost done. Before that, I'd focused entirely on the language of the prisoners, which was the big gap in the mainstream narrative of Abu Ghraib; yet I wanted to pull back a little, as in that photograph from the Abu Ghraib scandal where Ivan Frederick is visible looking down at a camera, in the foreground of the picture where the infamous picture of the hooded detainee is standing on a box with wires attached to his hands and feet. When that conversation could be seen— between official procedural discourse, soldier testimony, and detainee testimony—something larger emerged; it felt less like a poem of witness and more like a document of the war, writ large.

When I think of perversion at the heart of holiness, I return to Job, in which God makes a wager with Satan that Job will maintain his faith despite whatever suffering may befall him. So Satan takes away Job's family, wealth, friends, and physical health, stripping him of all worldly things. Job cries out in protest against his plight to God, and God's answer is something like, "I am mightier than you, mightier than you can imagine." Sound familiar? In other words, there is no ethical argument for Job's suffering. Job does not deserve it. It's one of the most frightening moments in the Bible, right up there with God's call to Abraham to sacrifice his son, or to the people to commit genocide in the Book of Samuel. This is a very flawed God, a Graner.

Which is why being a soldier puts one in the most difficult moral space; one is both Abraham and Isaac, at the same moment; the obedient one who listens to his commanding officer, and the one put in harm's way. And sometimes, that soldier is also God, in those moments where no God seems to be.

The immediacy of the incommensurable, mediated and yet unmediated, is what I was after in the arias. I wanted the reader to feel very strongly both the ways in which this text was a constructed thing, a borrowed thing, at the same time that it was marked by a human voice, struggling against all mediations.

MC: I did actually pick up on the SOP sections as the flip-side of the (echo /ex/) parts of the arias. The violence of the (echo / ex/)s definitely stands in opposition to the care demanded by the SOPs . . . care that is given to a book or a dead body, but not a person. For instance, we read in the SOPs:

thereby reducing the friction over searching

will avoid handling or touching

may or may not require a language

open

pages in an upright manner (as if reading[7]

Or:

like sandalwood

the whole body   a prayer

       folded

                   folded[8]

These sections are wonderful in how they show a concern with perfection on the part of the military couched in striking, sometimes musical and sometimes strange language. At the same time, the concern with perfection seems proper to art and ethics but is instead given to the handling of a book, a mere object, or a dead body, more than likely the body of someone killed by the same forces handling the dead man.

Another way the SOPs seem to operate in the arias is that they give us a glimpse of the conflicting directives given to soldiers. So, in "MUSLIM BURIAL" a body is a prayer arising out of the way the body is handled, or maybe the way we handle the body is the sort of prayer we make, or the body is a prayer in its amazing folded geometry, geometry found in its chemistry, its DNA. In the same poem, the same Standard Operating Procedure that directs a soldier to handle a body as a prayer, I find a cold diagram of how to prepare a burial trench . . . not at all prayer-like. The diagram is concerned with perfection, but perfection of action. A coldly formal perfection, maybe, that confuses the ethical description of the whole body [as] a prayer with the outward acts of prayer.

"Handling the Koran" also questions the conflicting rules soldiers must work under. It is almost as if the poem is organized in conflicts. The first line, avoid handling or touching challenges the last lines, handle "as if it were fragile / delicate art."[9] This repeats throughout the poem, so we get to open the one cover with one hand impossibly set against using two hands at all times, and the lines in an upright manner ("as if reading" is immediately followed by the order to ignore the text of the Koran) "if reading / not every page is to be."

Finally, there is the strange way the Koran is treated both with reverence and as an object of ridicule or danger. So we read, again from "Handling the Koran," that soldiers are to avoid "handling or touching / a language specific."[10] And earlier on, in "Searching the Koran," which implies the Koran is either being interrogated or is a source of intelligence regarding the enemy, we learn that "handling or touching / may or may not require a language / to open" and that "the book is / contours or protrusions / binding / the binding."[11] That is, the Koran is not a piece of culture to be appreciated and understood. It is a mere object made of leather and paper and ink. We can ignore reaching beyond our own view of the world, via Arabic and the Koran, and remain safely in our own language, English. So, again, while the SOPs demand perfect care, they also deny the value of what is handled.

In all of these contradictions, I continually wonder, what ethic guides our actions in war? If we go back to the notion of the sublime as a formless object that threatens to overwhelm us, then, in some way, war and its perversions are not perverse on their own level. But I do question what it means to talk about ethics at the level of war . . . as I think the arias do, in how they confront the difficulty of making sense of the perversion of holiness (that is to say, the difficulty of making sense of the notion of holiness as perverse and perverting the notion of holiness).

And maybe that is where your idea of witness or an account of war comes in. That is, the account is all that can be given. But then, where is the value of protest or opposition? Or is that the wrong question to ask when discussing the poetry of witness and the poetry of protest?

PM: I find myself rediscovering the poems through your readings of them; it's as if I were some sort of mole snuffling through the dirt of the words, and suddenly you open up a light into the tunnel, and I'm blind and I can see all at once.

That the poems have become a way to ask the questions—about ethics in war—seems to me the gift of a thoughtful and ethical reader, since too many of our conversations about poetry tend to reduce poetry to a series of language games or political gestures. When I was in Belfast with the peacebuilding class, a conversation blew up after our visit to the Police Service of Northern Ireland. One student, an ardent supporter of Irish independence, argued that during the independence movement, it was acceptable to order the killing of police, who were seen as British occupiers. Another student, the wife of a police officer, was appalled, and called him out on it. My colleague entered into the fray, and argued that it is never acceptable to kill anyone. I think my colleague was right, though his phrasing sounded as absolutist as the student sounded relativist. How can we not be disturbed by the killing of another human being? Can we ever say that it is acceptable? We may cede to its necessity, perhaps, but to call it acceptable feels like a sudden plunge into rationalization. We have talked Just War theory to death. We need new paradigms, such as Just Peacemaking, which aims to manage conflict before it comes to killing, and to adjudicate killing within the modes of restorative rather than retributive justice. It's all easy for me to say, however, from the safe distance of civilian life. Basically, we as citizens have failed our soldiers, when we have failed to brake imperial power, when we rationalize wars of convenience.

This leads to your question about whether poetry is the right medium to protest, to resist, and whether the witnessing function is in some sense more apt for poetry. *Behind the Lines* explores these questions, articulating a series of arguments for poetry as a mode of resistance, and a mode of resistance that is most fruitful when in dialogue with the peace movement and when it contains in itself a vision beyond resistance. I hesitate to boil it all down to a couple sentences, but that is a start. The question of efficacy is a torment, because we know of the seemingly inexorable powers of imperial war—but ours, at the bare minimum, is to refuse to justify the unjustifiable. As Herodotus wrote in his *Histories*, I write to prevent these deeds from drifting into oblivion, striving not only to chronicle what has happened but also articulate the contours and fleeting images of a more just, peaceful, sustainable world. Naomi Shihab Nye articulated this vision of belatedness and hope well in her poem "Jerusalem": it's late but everything comes next.

MC: I have been thinking about my original reactions to the poems in arias and your last note, especially your discussion of the heated debate between the student who saw it as acceptable to order the killing of police officers and the professor who declared killing is never acceptable. In some ways, this same

201

debate is present in me and in the arias. In "The Blues of Javal Davis," you write: "stay open about drawing an opinion ■■■ / ■■■■■■■■ from / the comforts of your living."[12] And I often sympathize with Davis' sentiment . . . I mean, things we do in war are very different from what we would find acceptable in day-to-day life. And we can't have war without those usually unacceptable acts, regardless of what people seem to believe regarding just war. (Or, at least, that is my take. We can't expect people to act like gentlemen when they are focused on dismembering each other.) Normally unacceptable acts are acceptable in times of war, assuming war is ever justified. QED. At the same time, when I was first reading the arias, I was taken in by the mixing of the victim's statements with the ancient, religious language, but stumbled when I came across "The Blues" sections. I read through "The Blues of Lane McCotter" as I would any other poem, taking in the multiple layers of meaning or ways of reading, thinking about how interesting it is that terms are blacked out but easily inferred from the context, reflecting on the ridiculousness of that sort of redaction. But when I read the Javal Davis poem, I thought about how stupid his character is . . . even though he is a real person. I was offended by his lame attempt at self-justification through the statement that others simply don't understand, as if that provides a justification rather than just shutting people off. I was offended by his argument that CNN says "were dumb / poor kids from Garbagecan USA / it didn't turn out to be that way," which, to me, indicated a complete lack of self-awareness, as Davis and the other soldiers at Abu Ghraib pretty much proved CNN correct.[13] But I was also offended, at first, by the implication that those soldiers represented soldiers, the implication that soldiers lack any sort of depth or music, beyond their pathetic attempts at singing the blues.

The thing is, I see most soldiers in the way I initially objected to [in the poem]. I remember soldiers telling stories about their tours in Iraq, how one sergeant I worked with recalled looking out over a crowd of civilians during some protest and wishing he could pull the trigger of his .50 caliber machine gun just so he could kill someone, or how another sergeant bragged about sabotaging a civilian's truck out in the middle of the desert just because the truck matched the description of an insurgent's vehicle. The soldier with the .50 caliber even admitted he would have pulled the trigger if his partner would have done so first, which called to mind "The Blues of Lynddie England" and her completely unbelievable denial of any sort of responsibility, as if she had been hypnotized.

No one really talks about the beautiful little girl who was always outside Cedar (a base in Iraq) when we pulled in from our missions early in the morning. The mindset is all about killing and proving yourself. But that is what war is. If I tell guys I thought the desert was beautiful or that really all I wanted to do was practice my Arabic (which didn't happen much at all), they always look at me as if I lost something.

That is "The Blues of Joe Darby." The military is rigged against anyone trying to live out the ideal of the gentleman soldier. Darby was outed and his life put at risk by the same Secretary of Defense who is supposed to enforce the regulations that Darby was attempting to adhere to. That is the way military life and ethics are structured. If your friend shoots into a crowd, you are expected to do so . . . or at least, you are expected not to say anything. At best, you kick his ass later on for being a hothead. (I often thought about what I would do if my guys stepped over the line. I think it would have been easier to kill them than to turn them in. Luckily, it never got that far, although some guys did get too twitchy for my own moral comfort when civilians got too close.) But if someone turns against the unit!

Actually, I was talking to an army doctor about these problems not all that long ago, saying that I hated working with these kinds of people, that I was tired of their view of the world. The response was similar to what you write in "The Blues of Ken Davis": "they say talk to a chaplain / they say it's all your perception / it's how you perceive."[14] But I did not have any sort of glamorous notion of America's Army when I joined . . . I just wanted to live the dream as we say. War was neither good nor bad to me . . . it just was. What I objected to wasn't due to a great shift in my moral perceptions, as the doctor suggested in an attempt to explain away my disgust with the people I worked with. My objection was to the contradiction between the quality of the people in the military as well as those in charge of it and the (probably impossible) ideal of the gentleman soldier who goes out to fight a war, regardless of its causes, in a way that demonstrates courage and a concern for honest humanity and a fascination with all aspects of life.

So my initial reading of the arias was a mixture of fascination at the uses of found texts and the melding of different sorts of language with a confused set of reactions that both recognized the depravity of the soldiers at Abu Ghraib and their all-too-common view of the enemy, as well as a knee-jerk desire to somehow complicate soldiers and defend them.

PM: I imagine that this last message had been working its way out of you for a little while, and I'm glad for it. At the same time that it enraged you for its moral relativism and excuse-making, "The Blues of Javal Davis" worked aesthetically and ethically for me as a kind of admonishment, to slow down my judgment, to remind myself that I should be careful that my personal distance from the atrocity of Abu Ghraib didn't become a shield from the morally complex position in which soldiers found themselves, and the range of responses to that moral complexity.

There was, in addition to Darby—the classic voice of conscience—a man named Joyner (the J of the poem), who would give a blanket to prisoners who had been stripped or beaten the night before. Joyner didn't blow the whistle as Darby had, but he did act humanely toward these prisoners. But could he have gone further? Maybe. But he knew, as Darby invariably knew, that crossing the line of silence would expel him forever from the brotherhood, the brotherhood and its conditional love.

So there are Darbys and Joyners and Davises and Graners, and each ultimately has to live with what they did. Some had to serve time in prison. And, of course, as we all know, there are the unnamed operatives who are culpable for acts not only of torture but also of murder who have borne no punishment, because they have acted with the blessing of the state. And, of course, this problem is not new to the Iraq War; Achilles rage at Agamemnon's abuse of power is what opens *The Iliad*.

Maybe you will be the writer to continue to complicate our vision of what soldiering is like, in ways that we civilians can only imagine.

MC: Maybe I am off here, but part of the challenge of the arias as I read them is how we treat linguistic and cultural artifacts. The method of the arias is to take words as building blocks, bits of syntax rather than semantic units . . . and the meaning arises after the bits are brought together as a whole. The prohibition not to translate word for word and the demand to skip lines are taken from one of the SOP sections of the arias, so it reflects a practical, military-oriented vision of meaning and language as a set of tools to communicate ACTIONABLE intelligence, which may be hidden within poems and proverbs, while the culture in its literary and linguistic forms is unimportant, irrelevant. That same set of rules at work in the SOP is also at work in the construction of the arias, but to a different effect, and that is the challenge. Where the SOP's intent is to translate letters, "not / analyze them," the arias wish to uncover meanings through working to further "clarify / names."[15] But the arias must first approach pieces of language as building blocks rather than bits that are meaningful on their own and untranslatable from one context to another. Which is, maybe, one of the fascinating aspects of language that poetry has worked to uncover . . . Language is at once completely void of fixed meaning and able to be reworked almost as we see fit, as well as forcing itself and its meanings on us as we see in the many-layered, polyphonic arias.

PM: Your reading of the arias is precisely what I hoped for. And your distinction—that the Standard Operating Procedure is centrally concerned with actionable intelligence, rather than cultural understanding—is the knife that separates the kind of thinking required of military intelligence and the intelligences outside of its ken. I'm reminded that my father, while teaching counterinsurgency after his active service in the Vietnam War (1967–68), focused on the writings of Ho Chi Minh; it was critical, the U.S. counterinsurgency theory went, to know the enemy . . . in order to win the war. Not to know the enemy to know the enemy, but to anticipate the enemy's future moves.

In the warrior tradition, there often was a great respect for the worthy enemy who demonstrated courage, because defeating such an enemy would make the victory more honorable (and even defeat, perhaps, less dishonorable). With modern war, technowar, bureaucratic drone war, insurgency/counterinsurgency, the enemy is reduced to body counts (or worse, not even worthy of counting). Similarly, the term actionable in this context means something that one might use for defeating the enemy. What is the opposite of actionable? The useless? The beautiful?

Actually, the original title of the arias was "u r arias." On this version's title page, the u and r are printed in the bold font, the rest is in ghost grayscale font; for me, the poem has always been a mirror in which we see ourselves. The way we look, and how we read, and what we do, reflect back upon us, whether we like it or not. We always hope our reading and our action move us outside of ourselves, but do they? Also, I hoped to echo the idea of an ur-text—all of the documents to which the poem points—which itself points back to the original Ur, one of the earliest cities of human civilization. As long as we have had writing, we've had laments about war, beginning with the Sumerian priestess Enheduanna's "Lament to the Spirit of War." Perhaps Thomas Merton was right: "that which is oldest is most young and most new. There is nothing so ancient and so dead as human novelty. . . . It is the very beginning itself, which speaks to us."[16]

Notes

1. Philip Metres, *Sand Opera* (Farmington, ME: Alice James Books, 2015), 13.

2. Ibid., 12.

3. Ibid., 8.

4. Ibid.

5. Robert E. Lee, letter to General P. G. T. Beauregard, October 3, 1865, quoted in John William Jones, *Life and Letters of Robert Edward Lee, Soldier and Man* (New York: Neale Publishing, 1906), 390.

6. Robert Hass, "Winged and Acid Dark," in *Time and Materials* (New York: Ecco Press, 2008), 11.

7. Philip Metres, *Sand Opera*, op cit., 15.

8. Ibid., 23.

9. Ibid., 15.

10. Ibid.

11. Ibid., 7.

12. Ibid., 9.

13. Ibid., 9.

14. Ibid., 21.

15. Ibid.

16. Thomas Merton, *New Seeds of Contemplation* (New York: New Directions, 2007), 107.